THE ISSUE IS 'ISM

Women of Colour Speak Out

Fireweed's Issue 16

Sister Vision

Black Women and Women of Colour Press

ISBN 0-920813-72-0

Originally published by *Fireweed, A Feminist Quarterly* in 1983,
this edition of *Fireweed's Women of colour,* Issue 16 is published
by Sister Vision Press.

Cover: Stephanie Martin
Cover Photograph: Maria LaYacona
Typesetting: Hindsight
Printed by Union Labour at Our Times

Canadian Cataloguing in Publication Data

The Issue is 'ism: Women of colour speak out

Reprint. Originally published as issue 16 of Fireweed with special
title: Women of colour.
Includes bibliographical references.
ISBN 0-920813-72-0

1. Minority women – Canada – Literary collections.
2. Minority women – Canada. 3. Canadian literature (English) –
Minority authors.* 4. Canadian literature (English) – Women
authors.* 5. Canadian literature (English) – 20th century.*
I. Gupta, Nila. II. Silvera, Makeda, 1955- .

PS8235.W7188 1989 C810'.8'09287 C89-095456-9
PR9194.5.W6188 1989

Published by
SISTER VISION
Black Women and Women of Colour Press
P.O. Box 217, Station E
Toronto, Ontario
Canada M6H 4E2

Contents

The Issue is 'Ism

This book first appeared in the 1983 Issue 16 of *Fireweed, A Feminist Quarterly*, Toronto, Canada. It was the first time in Canadian feminist literature that women of colour collectively came together to talk in a single anthology. The powerful collection includes essays, short stories, poems, photographs and graphics by Black women, Asian women, Native women. Sisters from the Philippines and Central America also speak out. They speak of relevant issues facing women of colour the world over: racism, sexism, classism, imperialism and other 'isms.

When issue 16 first hit the stands, it was a collection of radical work in the minds of many readers; and both its development and presentation caused quite a debate particularly in the white women's literary community.

For many women of colour Issue 16 of Fireweed was testimony to their lived reality and dramatically illustrated their experiences as non-white women living in this society.

Sister Vision Press is pleased to reprint this historical and still relevant anthology.

Sister Vision Press
September, 1989

We Were Never Lost

We would like to share with our readers how this issue of Fireweed, Women of Colour, came to be. About two years ago Makeda Silvera and Dionne Brand approached the Fireweed Collective with the suggestion of an issue on women of colour. But, after a number of frustrating and fruitless meetings with the collective, we gave up the idea of guest editing an issue on the theme for Fireweed.

After nearly a year and a half, members of the collective came to us to ask us to work on an issue on women of colour. We were puzzled. "Why now?" we wondered. Our past dealings with the collective had been marked by their refusal to acknowledge that women of colour should have full editorial control over the production of an issue which would explore our lives. We found the invitation racist in fact if not in intent. We had questions. Did Fireweed now feel the climate was right? Was it now "politically correct" to devote an issue to women of colour? Would this issue be seen as "taking care of" the matter? Having been "discovered" by white feminists would women of colour then see the repetition of an herstorical pattern within the feminist movement which has consistently dealt with our concerns in a token fashion at best and most often not at all?. Despite our doubts, we decided, in collaboration with Nila Gupta, Himani Bannerji and Prabha Khosla, to guest edit this issue. We decided to use this medium, first to reach out to women of colour and second, to educate white feminists.

So often we hear women's publications, presses and organizations excuse all white publications and groups with he cry that they cannot "find" women of colour. We were never lost. And, as you will note in this issue, we are not invisible. On the contrary, we are alive and living in Canada.

The process of creating this issue took ten months of work under draining and often acrimonious conditions. Shortly after we put our wheels into motion two members of our collective temporarily left the country - Himani Bannerji to do research in Calcutta for her thesis and Dionne Brand to work in revolutionary Grenada. Nonetheless, we decided collectively to do whatever it took to pull the issue together. We continued to work through letters, telegrams and phone calls.

We spent hours reading and re-reading submissions, working on manuscripts, replying to countless letters and phone calls, making the often difficult decisions about what we would publish. It was an exciting and rewarding experience, but a tiring one because the unpaid labour we put into it came on top of our other daily commitments - our families, our jobs, our academic pursuits. We wish that as a working collective we had more time to meet. The demands in our personal and political lives did not permit this. We hope that through this issue we'll come together, meet new women of colour, and share our lives and our visions.

We also think it important to share with our readers how we "found" the women of colour who contributed to this issue. We distributed flyers with a covering letter inviting writers and non-writers from all over the country to submit manuscripts. We sent flyers to feminist publications, but this was not our main target group. We sent flyers to many ethnic publications, to organizations of women of colour, to interval houses, to the prisons. We posted flyers in shopping areas, laundromats, restaurants, book stores, day care centres, universities and other places women of colour are to be found. We used personal contacts and word of mouth to get the word out. In short, we tried and succeeded in reaching women outside the so-called feminist network.

Our criteria was that contributions be from women of colour and be on their experiences as women or as visible peoples. What we selected for publication was chosen according to a combination of artistic and political standards. Our major concern was to choose works that communicated. But we made a conscious decision to reject white male literary standards which have been used to still the voices of peoples of colour of both sexes. For this issue we tried to select a wide range of works with which to demonstrate the diversity within the community of women of colour - fiction, prose poetry, graphics, photography, personal experiences, political commentary, book reviews. In a number of pieces the names are deliberately left off. These include a testimony form a woman from Fiji who has been the survivor of numerous assaults by her husband and who eventually left him to start a new life successfully, the reflections of a young Black lesbian feminist, a taped discussion between three lesbians of colour, and the reflections of a West Indian domestic worker. That these women must remain nameless is a sad commentary on white-dominated society and male supremacy, and on their respective communities.

We wish we had received submissions from women of colour in prisons. We wanted articles form older women of colour dealing with their lives and on ageism/racism. We had also hoped for articles on women of colour and the health care system, and from teenagers and young women of colour, particularly between the ages of sixteen and twenty-one. We hope that these topics will emerge in other publications by women of colour.

But even with these limitations, this Women of Colour issue is herstoric in Canada. It is the first work of its kind to be published here. We expect that this issue will be relevant for many years to come. We hope that women's studies programmes and the feminist press will take advantage of the unique material we have brought together. We think it important that what is between these pages become a way for the teachers of women's studies and women's publishers to begin to inform themselves about the lives of women of colour.

Finally, we would like to thank everyone who contributed to bring this issue form idea to reality. We deeply admire the courage and dedication of those women who could not sign their names, but were determined to share their lives with us.

Makeda Silvera
Nila Gupta
Managing Editors for the Fireweed Guest Collective

We Appear

Silent

To People

Who Are

Deaf

To What

We Say

Race and the Limits of Sisterhood

Makeda: I'm really sick of some of these white feminists when they talk about rape. It's always from *their* perspective - being knocked down somewhere is a dark alley or a park and being raped. They never mention other kinds of rape, other abuse that women of colour and immigrant women experience, like men hassling you on the bus or train at night, calling you names, the day to day social rape... A couple of nights ago I was waiting for the train and this drunk guy, big redneck, came up and started shouting, "Bitch! Bitch!" There was me and two other guys waiting for a train and he's shouting out "Bitch! Bitch!" I'm really frightened because this guy is really big and I'm wondering what would happen if he came up and attacked me physically. What was I going to do? This white woman walks up on the platform and he starts up again. We kind of look at each other in solidarity and I feel less scared because at least there is another woman. But then, this drunk started calling out, "Nigger! Nigger!" and looking directly at me. That woman, she just looked right through me and there wasn't that kind of connection, that solidarity, anymore. It was really frightening. I didn't know what to do. I was angry, I was filled with rage, I wanted to attack the man, I wanted to cry, and suddenly I felt really embarrassed. I didn't know why.

Dionne: I know how it is, I know that feeling.

Himani: So, while the whole thing was about women, when he was calling you "bitch," she was ready to relate to you. But as soon as your race came into focus, she too went over to the other side and didn't identify with you any more. So, in some sense, the women's movement in Canada is mainstream and does not seek to identify with women of colour.

Dionne: It doesn't address other issues that concern women of colour.

Himani: There is also the whole question of the book *Still Ain't Satisfied! Canadian Feminism Today* (Women's Press, 1982). It claims to anthologize the experiences of women in the movement for the last ten years in Canada, but actually leaves women of colour and immigrant women under-represented... We are made invisible in the mainstream. And there is talk about "coming from the woman's perspective, coming from the woman's standpoint." It seems to me very empty, this standpoint, because I do not know who this woman is that they are talking about. It never comes down to a specific group of women. They talk about women as a empty category. They will not talk about women as class, about a particular type of woman, about woman as race, so it leaves you very empty at the end.

Dionne: In *Immigrant Housewives in Canada: A Report* (sponsored by Immigrant Women's Centre, 1981), they link the struggle of immigrant women to struggle in the house, to the husband taking away her right to speak and so on, which is bullshit.

Class and the Limits of Sisterhood

Himani: Vast numbers of immigrant women work outside the home all the time. Even in terms of house work, they do this in other people's houses as domestic workers.

Dionne: If one were to identify immigrant women, black women, women of colour with the aspect of domestic work in the home, it would perhaps represent 25 per cent. The other 75 per cent would be...

Prabha: ...struggles of living within this society.

Himani: I'm concerned with the emptiness of that concept "woman." It has nobody in it. If you want to pin it down to anybody, it is a very middle class woman - a graduate student dropping out of graduate school with some prospect of intellectual or other employment - if not now, at some point - a woman living alone with a particular lifestyle that is highly cultured, who has access to what is denied most people.

Makeda: Even then, there is no voice of working class white women. It's all very middle-Canada.

Dionne: Precisely. I was also wondering if there is any representation of white working class women in the book *Still Ain't Satisfied*?

Prabha: There is stuff around the clerical workers, the bank tellers.

Makeda: That is what they always classify as working class and that is where their working class consciousness stops.

Dionne: What about the piece workers in the factories? What about the labourers?

Makeda: What about women of colour, immigrant women in factories and the difficulty of organising unions there? Nothing. It's like our experiences are not valued. Our experiences in organising and becoming part of unions are varied, particularly because of our being immigrants, where the fear of deportation is ever present - and the other immigrant women in factories, whose first language is not English.

Himani: They are always saying - and I think *Immigrant Housewives in Canada* is a good example of it - that immigrant women are silent. I don't think that immigrant women are silent. You appear silent to people who are deaf to what you say.

Prabha: They have their own idea of what we should be saying and until we say those things they pretend to be deaf.

Himani: So, if you don't fit into that, then as far as they're concerned, you're not saying anything. And, they have a particular way of deciding what they'll count as "saying," and that "saying" is not how we speak.

Dionne: As a matter of fact, I think they like us like that - not "saying." They like us to join with them and struggle with them - but just as a symbol. We don't even have to say anything. It's worth it to them if we are completely illiterate or at least appear that way. You don't have to say anything as long as they can get a few women of colour and immigrant women out to a demonstration. That's wonderful, because symbolically we've always meant some kind of radical idea.

Himani: But, also, we've legitimised what they are doing by going there. But, I think the other question about even illiterate people is not that they don't say things, it's *how* they say it. There is only one way of "saying" that counts. In that sense, they are forcing all the most middle class, the most male bourgeois ways of speaking and doing things on us. And if you don't do things that way, then you're not doing it, you're not "saying" it right. What I challenge is this whole notion of the silence of people.

Prabha: It's also because a lot of the women in the women's movement are fairly well-educated and have a university education, so they have writing skills. Because we don't write, they cannot read our articles, and they figure that we don't have experience, or that we don't exist as coloured women who are actively organised.

Makeda: I would even challenge that. There are many of us who write, they just don't want to read it; they don't want to publish it. Reading and publishing our work would definitely force white women to look at themselves, at racism and at what has been laid on us for years. The latest issue has been how patriarchal our culture is and how male-identified women of colour and immigrant women are. We are labelled male-identified every time we talk about struggling with Third World men to end racism and imperialism. This view of the world and the relationship of peoples in the world is certainly not compatible with mine.

Dionne: Any immigrant woman/woman of colour analyzing her situation in the world has to analyze it beyond the point of being a woman, because there are other people who are in the same condition and some of them are men. We cannot analyze the world as though men of colour are not oppressed too, because that way of analyzing the world gives us no way out of it.

I think there would be a place for serious struggle if you did have a class analysis, if that analysis was based on real issues, on the real way you live. If it isn't - if you have to organize as women - middle class women, upper class women, poor women - then those various interests are never going to form a coherent voice because our economic conditions will never be addressed.

Himani: White feminists don't want to deal with issues of race and class within the feminist movement. So if you're a woman of colour, what do you do? Just struggle at home with our husbands and lovers?

Dionne: It's always on a personal level, or you accept the state as it is and then you go after little bits of rights. You leave the state intact and merely say, "If you give me this reparation here and that reparation there, then it will be o.k." But you don't attack the whole framework, which is a class framework.

Himani: But, if they are going to have woman's perspective, divorced from a class or a socialist perspective, then we're going to have to fight with them, too. It's like apartheid in South Africa - you fight against apartheid, not just the men in South Africa.

Dionne: But, how does a women's movement fight in a place like South Africa?

Prabha: There isn't a women's movement. There are white women's organizations like Black Sash. They've done some good work in their capacity as white women, but there is not a Black women's organization as such. The word "feminism", is not identifiable even though there are a lot of women struggling who we would call "feminists" because of how they operate in society. Political organizations do have women's caucuses - but you can't organize in that society on that basis; you're too worried about bread and butter issues. How can you fight for women's rights alone in a society where nobody who is Black has rights?

Himani: When you go into a room full of people and you see them all different from you, and really benefitting from the power structure and protecting their particular interests - both men and women - how do you identify with the women in that room? - when you know what's happening to your people is benefitting them. The Angela Davis book, *Women, Race and Class,* really concretised this for me. Basically, what she said was that you cannot free people in parts; you cannot take the Black woman and free her when Blacks as a whole do not hold any economic and social position in this particular society.

Makeda: I'm going to play the devil's advocate. Are we saying there's no place for Black feminism?

Dionne: No, not at all. We're saying we have to take other things into consideration. As a matter of fact, I think white women should take other things into consideration, too.

Makeda: White women have to deal with that, too. I'm tired of carrying around their dead weight and easing their guilt complexes.

Himani: As Black feminists we have lot of problems. I think we have a more complex situation that white women because we fight with one hand tied behind our backs. We feel very attacked by the society at large. At times, this makes it very hard for us to turn in our men to this society, which is whipping us all to be whipped even further. Yet, at home we have horrible relationships. These men not only have patriarchal values, but they take out the pressures from the society on us. So we are holding two social positions that are very oppressive. We pay for somebody else being kicked around; we get kicked around ourselves. At the same time, we can't politically hand people over from our community to other people's to be punished. We are stuck with having to formulate a movement which is even more complex than anything we could ever dream of. When you are in your own society with no question of racism or imperialism between the two sexes, then you can really freely fight out the fight of patriarchy. But here, our fight with patriarchy is really compounded with the issue of racism. The women's movement here is historically unable to state that position, because it isn't their headache - except politically in an intellectual sense of the word - a moral commitment. At home, when the fight a white man, they don't fight imperialism.

Dionne: They don't fight patriarchy. In fact, they are fighting for a piece of the stuff, a piece of the action. It's the same thing as the Black Power movement in the '60s and '70s. I got caught up in Black nationalism. You saw the entire race moving in some direction and didn't differentiate between the middle class and you, because you thought whatever you were able to get, all of us had in some way. It's not true. We have different interests. Some Black middle class person has completely different interests than me. His interest is in keeping the state going as is, just getting his own.

Himani: You feel it's the same thing in the women's movement?

Dionne: Yes, there's a kind of feminist nationalism. Some woman who lives in Don Mills with a job as a manager - her interests are different from mine. She is most likely satisfied with how the place is being run and only wants a piece of it. Me, I'm not satisfied with how it runs at all, and I don't want a piece of it either. I want it completely put together and divided up some other way.

Rape and the Myth of the Black Savage

Dionne: What is also interesting is the issue of rape. Angela Davis talks about it as it applies to Blacks and Black women. Rape has always been used in America and here against Black men, and it's very, very tricky for us. Of course we feel the same way about rape as white women do, but I'm always suspicious when I hear of a Black man raping a white woman.

Prabha: Do you remember that happening last summer here in Toronto? There was this composite picture in the newspaper of this Black guy - dreadlocks. Then three months down the road the picture changed. He was white - he just had curly hair. He had gone to a salon before the rape.

Dionne: But the picture was white, for godsake! They said first of all that it was a Black man, a Rasta who had raped the woman in High Park. Then the picture changed and they said he was a mulatto. Then it started to change (*laughter*). Soon he was octoroon, quadroon, and he was white six months later.

Makeda: During that period, whenever I was around white women and the rape came up I felt really isolated. I felt that I couldn't discuss the rape and the rapist with them because this man was supposed to be Black and I'm Black. This man was supposed to be a Rastafarian and I am a Rastafarian. Somehow, I felt they had stopped seeing me as a woman; I was now Black and Rastafarian - devoid of sex. For them, the central issue seemed to be his Blackness. I felt that to partake in that racist discussion would be saying something against my race. He simply wasn't a man who raped a woman. He was Black and she was white. He was not a man, he was not a person who had committed a crime, just Black, Black, and that made me really uncomfortable. I feel connected to this person because he's Black and because we live in a racist society and I'm reminded of that every day, every hour of my life.

Himani: In fact, what they were doing was replaying the whole myth...

Makeda: ...a Black, a savage, a wild Black. He may have been a Black man, but that is irrelevant. We knew as soon as that came out that it would reinforce the myth.

Dionne: Not only that, but he would then be responsible for all the rapes, before and after. This depravity, this person violating white womanhood - the whole business all over again.

Makeda: When they had that demonstration to protest the rape, you didn't know whether the women who were demonstrating were out there protesting because it was a Black savage. I remember I really wanted to go, but I was hesitant. I wondered whether half of the people who had gone went to demonstrate against this Black that they wanted to find and kill. This might not have been foremost in their minds, but I can't help thinking that it might have been at the back.

Himani: There are two ways of spreading that myth - to be openly racist and say Black men rape - and the other which comes from a very weird, distorted guilt feeling I've noticed in a few white women. There was an incident where someone said, "But, we have so badly treated Black people that when they come in contact with our women, our children, we should expect violence from them." So it comes from guilt, but the guilt produces an incredible amount of racism!

The Shaping of Consciousness

Prabha: In South Africa it's a different story because race and class are like this: you're upper class and you're white, and you're poor and you're Black.

Dionne: I know what you mean. Race and class are synonymous in Trinidad.

Himani: In Canada, would you say race and class are not synonymous? Is there a lot of leeway?

Dionne: I think ultimately it is. I certainly have difficulty with some people in my own community about race...

Makeda: ...and about class.

Prabha: In the East Indian community we have to deal with the problems of class because even if a lot of people aren't necessarily wealthy, they still do this upper class number.

Makeda: I know the trips they put themselves through. Some people from the West Indies come here and after a year or two try to change their entire identity. Suddenly you hear that they are from upper middle class families in the Caribbean, own plantations, have maids...

Dionne: Suddenly they've become assistant-whites (*laughter*).

Makeda: This divides us more than anything else - even working with other women - other women of colour who have all these grand aspirations and fantasies to be like their bosses and in turn oppress and harass other women. How can I work with them?

Prabha: I make class lines. She might be Chinese, she might be Black, and if she's upper class and not on the side of working class people, that's where I draw the line.

Dionne: I remember Makeda wrote this article on domestic workers and it appeared in *Spear Publications* while I was working there. One woman who owned a beauty parlour and who probably came as a domestic worker called up the publisher and said, "But we must forget these things, we can't keep harping on these things all the time." She was very upset that the article was in the magazine.

Himani: That fear has to be looked into. I don't think that because certain people don't want to talk about those past experiences means that they have upward aspirations. They may, but that's beside the point. They don't want to be noticed; they want to be left alone and unobtrusively inch their way forward. They know that if you are noticed too much you're liable to be attacked. What they are doing is adopting this animal principle of protective colouring, camouflaging themselves quietly in the environment. That comes not because they hope for very much here, but because they know how hard it is. There was that shooting in the courtroom where an East Indian man allegedly shot two other men. I went that same day to Gerrard Street (where several East Indian establishments are located) to eat. I was talking with the people who owned the restaurant and they were really angry. They said, "This fucker! Why did he have to do something that has brought so much attention to us? He's playing radical and he's off somewhere safe. We have businesses, we have children and we will get the police coming down on us." The situation is weird. You come from somewhere obviously with class problems and poverty (let's leave for a moment who creates them). You come here with a degree and so forth. Even with a degree a middle class Black on the street is visibly seen as working class. Black is worker, Black is matched to labour. She may be a doctor, she may be a professor. It makes no difference at all. You are Black and you are immediately slotted. Once your hopes are broken, you may identify with what's going on, with being called working class - feel it and fight for it. Or, it may further reinforce reactionary behaviour - make you start glorifying a nostalgic India so everything about that country, including its completely reaction- ary traditions and trends, are glorified. The community freezes as a culture and also becomes repressive. Through fear you don't want to be noticed. You know you don't have a revolution on your doorstep; there are no important unions or political parties that give a shit about what happens to other people who come to this country. You know you've got to fend for yourself. You are not going to play any radical games. You're going to lie low, be quiet and work hard and hope to die without being noticed or hurt by anybody - unlike Albert Johnson (shot in his Toronto home by the police). Third, you ally here with the Liberal and Conservative political parties.

Makeda: It's the same in the Black community. Our parents love the Liberal government because they opened the doors for Black people to come here.

Himani: So, the effects of imperalism and capitalism are seen not only in directly oppressing you by calling you a bitch on the street or slotting you in a particular kind of job. It's done by actually distorting the existence of a whole group of people here through fear tactics and devices, within which it contains you. You cannot help but respond, and what you respond as and become is an utterly reactionary person, which is where all the total uncaringness and racism within the political parties and the trade unions becomes an important issue.

Prabha: People are scared. They don't know how it works here and they don't want to challenge too much even if they're getting beat to the ground because who knows, maybe they'll have to go back home or life could get worse.

Himani: Where the hell will they go back to? You're forty, you have kids and you left a job and sold everything to buy a plane ticket to come here.

Dionne: The other things the immigrant category does to you is stop you from looking at you real relations to thing. You are not a worker anymore, you no longer have rights because you're here by somebody's largesse, like Trudeau's. You feel you don't have rights and you shouldn't speak out. You belong to the Liberal party simply because they opened the doors for you. You stop relating to yourself in terms of the work you do, the taxes you pay, the rights you have. You don't feel you should ask for anything. It's a nice deal. There's a non-politicised workforce that doesn't see its relation to the work it does.

How Things Get Done...Or How Can I Play by the Rules If I Don't Know What They Are?

Himani: Is there a particular way of getting things done in this society that the women's movement shares?

Dionne: There was a thing in the '70s about working differently than men. They formed themselves into co-operatives, and so on, but the co-operatives have been falling apart ever since, and more and more women's organisations are moving from that to working in the same kind of structure as men.

Prabha: I've been working in women's organisations for years and I think there has been a serious attempt to try and have structures that are quite contrary to hierarchical, patriarchal structures. That is something we do not have in our history that we can build from. At the same time, there are things that are quite manipulative of immigrant women. On the one hand, you rotate chairs, minute taking, and so on, so that there will be some level of skill sharing between all members of the collective. There are clearing sessions where people can talk about how one person got to monopolize the chair. So there is some room to raise issues, but there are unspoken leaders, and there are the ones that go on and on about how we are collective and should make decisions together. You know there are leaders, but it's totally behind the scenes. I feel that these women do manipulate the young, new, naive women in the group. You have to know how to talk like them, you have to be articulate, you have to know when to raise your voice.

Dionne: Or, if you bring up an issue that is basic and working class, then they will say, "Well, but, we have to look at something else."

Makeda: No, no. (*laughter*) They will say really fast, "Yes, yes, that's an important issue, we have to work on it," and then it's forgotten.

Himani: Do people get you to say things they they want you to say by asking certain kinds of questions?

Prabha: Sometimes when they ask things I get an answer from them before I can say what I think!

Your Models Don't Match Our Reality

Prabha: Some women were trying to organise an Indian women's group, but I don't think that they had really worked much around the Indian community or with women. They were advertising in all sorts of lefty journals about how they were starting this Indian women's group and that they were going to have meetings. They were advertising in lefty feminist newspapers and I didn't thing that that was what Indian women were reading. I kept saying to them that maybe we should be writing little stories about our lives in Canada and our oppression as women in our cuture - in Indian newspapers. It was never done. Then they leafletted the bazzikie parade, a Sikh religious parade - that's a big family thing, not the place to leaflet. Also, you do not leaflet Indian women; that is not how you talk to Indian women. They did a lot of things like that, which to me was a real male, left-white-working-class-men's tactic, and here they were trying to organise Indian women. So I said that what we had to do was to go down to the bodwars, go down and sit with the women, eat with them, go meet them face to face and talk - meet in our homes and get to know each other.

Makeda: It seems to me that they were coming from a very middle class perspective, a middle class way of organising working class women which almost always fails.

Dionne: You live a protected life like that. They are not going to get the same kind of reaction as working class Indian women.

Himani: You know, I was educated in India, but obviously not in the proper direction of learning how liberal democracy works. It's a country where we haven't figured out all those things yet. It's (*laughter*) brute coercion or being left along. It's not a welfare state. An occupation like social worker I had never heard of until I came here. And in India, there's not this idea of dividing politics into community politics, national politics and international politics.

When I came here, one of the things I didn't know was how meetings were conducted. I had never heard of "Robert's Rules" so I didnt' know you had to speak through the chair. You couldn't come in and just say what you wanted to say. I was rendered completely neutralised, completely powerless by the structure of the meeting.

Prabha: Working class Canadian women can't relate to that either.

Himani: Well, I think that we have been part of a movement which is called the women's movement - it needs no membership. But to organise for them means to organise in a certain way, to speak for them means to speak in a certain language. Organisations mean a certain set of procedures, and so on. People come in without knowing any of that and then they say to you, "You know, you haven't spoken," or "You don't know how to do it," when to do it is to do it in a certain way. I think we are squeezed out because we don't know how to use the liberal apparatus.

Makeda: We are people of colour and we remain as foreigners, even after being in this country for over fifteen or twenty years.

Prabha: One white woman came up to me and said she wanted to write short stories about our oppression for us to read because most of the things that are out on the market are to hard, too intellectual for us to read. This is supposed to be a feminist?!

Makeda: Nila, what is your experience? You're not an immigrant.

Nila: No, not in the literal sense. My mother was visiting her parents in Montreal when she had me, so I'm Canadian by birth, though all my siblings are Indian by birth. The first six years of my life were lived in India, and then my family immigrated to Canada. Coming to Canada was a shock, a rude one, but I was young so I adapted. The fact that my mother is white also helped to cushion the shock. My identity is Indian, but my experience is largely Canadian. When I walk down the street or into a room, the first thing anyone ever asks me is, "What is your nationality/race?"

Himani: You are partly Indian and partly French Canadian, how are you perceived by mainstream Canadian feminists?

Nila: They don't know exactly where to place me but they do know that I'm "different." Because I'm partly white, I'm considered less intimidating. If you and I went to a meeting they would accept me more readily that they would accept you because they assume that I'm assimilated, that I come from a white person's perspective and, to a certain extent, they are right. I have had that hammered in me.

Makeda: Does that mean that they can talk about women of colour objectified with you present? Not that they don't do it with me! (*laughter from Dionne and Himani*)

Nila: Yes, because they do feel a bit less intimidated.

Prabha: They also say things like, "I never think of you as that." It's like we're invisible.

Nila: They use me in a very dangerous way because they recognise (or hope) that I have been silenced, and I am visibly different. When I walk in they have their token member, but they know, "Oh, she's gonna be silent, she's not going to cause problems." So it's very convenient for them to have me there, I think. They can be "politically correct" and continue in the same fashion undisturbed, unchanged and comfortable.

Prabha: It's really hard to be the only coloured woman in a group and continuously raise the same issues. It would be extremely difficult for me.

Himani: We're made invisible in two ways: one is by not being allowed into the mainstream, not getting published, not getting recognised. Last night, at a conference on lyric poetry at the University of Toronto - an all North American white conference - this guy, who is a left critic, and a couple of other people came up to me and said, "Oh, it's wonderful, you know you have really revived my notion of good aesthetics..." Now what I want to ask them is, "Why don't you ever organise anything? We're here. These people read in lots of places; you never go there, you never make it possible, you don't publish them, you don't review their books, and yet this evening out of nowhere you come in, you hear us, and then you say, "How fantastic!"

Dionne: He's slumming... We're going uptown to hear jazz. (*Makeda laughs*)

Himani: You are rendered invisible by the fact that there is no place for you in the mainstream; they will not organise a place for you, but they will make this little excursion into slum life. (*Makeda laughs*)

Those of us who work with community workers, social workers, agencies of different kinds, are stuck with being invisible in a different way. It's, "You are one of us," but we are *not* "one of us." When they are sitting there discussing "them" - the immigrant women - and telling you in front of you that they are "them," what they are doing is denying your whole existence, and saying you don't have those problems, as though outside of that room, you don't have another existence, as if you don't send your kids to school, or try to make a living.

Prabha: To get called "punjab" on the street - they don't have to live with that.

Dionne: Or, let us say one of them, quite liberal, decides to make a stab at trying to meet with women of colour. They call three, four or five people, and nobody appears. (*laughter*) They give up, disillusioned (*laughter*); they now have a whole theory about who we are and everything else. After they have tried to contact three or four of us, and we don't come, they now feel that we are not interested, that we are not political, that we are not all kinds of things.

Getting On With It

Prabha: The question is: What are we going to do with a women's movement that is mostly white? We are all feminists and we work in our own communities. I'm tired of going on about how they don't do this and how they never speak for us.

Makeda: But we don't want them to speak for us. What do they know about our oppression? I'm saying that they *do* have a responsiblity if they claim that they are feminist and political. They have to struggle on all levels and *not* just around what is of primary concern to them. I am saying that they have to take responsibility for their white skin privilege, take responsibility for the power they wield in this society. Do we have a women's press? Can we publish our own stuff? Who controls the women's presses? Isn't it white women who claim to be feminist and "politically correct"? Well, if that is so, then they have responsibility to work to create a new vision of the world which includes women of colour.

Prabha: But what is our role? What is it that we are going to do and how are we going to work: Are we going to work in our own structure, in our communities and at some point will this women of colour/immigrant women's movement meet with the white women's movement and hash it out?

Lillian: I think that they benefit objectively from our oppression.

Dionne: You're damn right.

Lillian: And they have to be called on that, they have to struggle with that.

Himani: I still think that Prabha's point is very well taken. Let's say that solidarity work is possible. If it is possible between different countries, it's possible in the same city with different groups. But - other than the unconscious and conscious imperialisms, middle class techniques and methods of organisation that these people hold, and their class backgrounds - there is also the historical inability on the part of people raised in Downsview (a Toronto suburb) to try to stand in for people coming from somewhere else. It's neither desirable nor possible. But there could be under-standing, as we understand people from other parts of the world. I think it is really incumbent upon us to organise.

Makeda: We are not disagreeing on that. I know that that is necessary, that we have to come together as a people, as a race, and organise. But that does not let white women off the hook; they have a responsibility to work out their shit and not to oppress us with it.

Himani: Something that bothers me about the women's movement is that they continuously talk about *men*. I am sick and tired of talking about men; I don't want to hear about men. I want to hear about women and what is happening to them, and, if necessary, bring in certain aspects of how men relate to this.

Our Lives Are More Than Just Problems

Prabha: In Vancouver, the Women's Studies Association was going to have a conference - they are all white, white. So they phone Nyga, who is Jamaican and a friend of mine, and ask her if she could do something on women in the Third World and health. Then they call me up. So Nyga and I are supposed to have *the* word on women and health and the Third World. I don't like that. I tell them that there are Indian women who are doctors in town who were probably doctors in India and to talk to them.

Dionne: It's not part of their struggle, not part of the way they organise.

Prabha: But we are not just this one little thing that can be wrapped up in one session.

Dionne: This reminds me of a paper I did on images of Third World peoples in the press in advanced capitalist countries. Go though three quarters of any major newspaper and it's *their* lives, *their* politics, *their* murders, *their* births, *their* deaths, *their* everything. Then, there is one page on the Third World, and it is all about floods, hurricanes, brutality, political struggle, tribalism, cannibalism, all on one page. *Their* lives have a sequence, have moments, differences, nuances. Within the structure of capitalism what they do is connect their way of living with being worthwhile and then they disjoint it, dismember it from *your* way of living. So there are no *people* in the Third World: there are floods, famines, brutality, cannibalism, tribalism and so on. There are no people who live from morning to morning, with lives that have sequences. What this does is keep us where we are and them where they are.

Prabha: That's like having a conference with one speaker to speak for twenty minutes on Third World issues and Third World women. It depersonalises you. You're not an individual who laughs and cries, but has happy moments too. You're suddenly a member of a wretched group that never laughs, never shares good times, for in that twenty minutes all we can talk about are the problems of Third World women.

Dionne: That sort of thing disembodies you. You are a thing, you are not a person who lives from day to day. You only live the problems.

Himani: That is an emptying out of any historical, daily, concrete, specific class experience so what is left is this empty thing into which everything is filled.

Dionne: And most of the things that fill it are problems: we don't get along, we don't have husbands, we don't have children, we only have burdens. Or children are seen only as burdens because they have to be fed: they are not a joy to lie with and look at.

We Know What We're Doing

Himani: There's also a whole big craze about genital mutilation.

Dionne: Oh my god, give me a break! I've heard that over and over again!

Himani: Why are they so interested? I'm not saying it's a great practice....

Prabha: In Copenhagen, at the women's conference, it came up. White women really got it because Third World women just told them to get off. They said, "We know what we are doing, we're working on it, and we don't need you to tell us how to do things. Besides, look at your culture and all the psychological oppression. Look at your high-heeled shoes and your clothes, and then tell us that genital mutilation is so much worse than what you have."

Makeda: The presumption is that the women whose lives it affects are not doing any work around genital mutilation, are not talking about it.

Prabha: What it also says is that our cultures are more sexist than their's. For example, I hate to talk about doweries with white women because they think our culture is so sexist. They have no idea where that fits into society, how it originated, where it came from.

Who are the Women in Struggle?

Lillian: When I used to move around with some people from the left - were they ever out in left field - I always had problems when they talked about the West Indies or the Jamaican situation. They would talk about these backward countries, these backward people, but when I reflect on it, the Third World is the only place where there have been revolutions.

Prabha: That's also where the white women's movement gets its role models - the women with guns, the women fighting are Vietnamese, Nicaraguan, Chinese women, not lily-white women. Yet nobody has said point-blank, "Look who our heroines are."

Himani: I was in a conference two weeks ago where they were talking about how *we* come from a more patriarchal background than *they* come from ....

Makeda: Oh yeah, tell me more. I'm sick and tired of hearing that one. I think I am going to bodily harm to the next white woman who tries to convince me of that. (*laughter*)

Himani: (*laughter*) We cannot speak up. We haven't got education; we cannot be expected to live on Canadian taxpayers' money, to get into jobs that they are paying for, and so on. The question is: Who is a Canadian? You are an immigrant, you have citizenship, so who is Canadian? And this image of "backwardness," of a complete inability on our part to stand up and yet ....

Makeda: But who are the women who pick up guns? Who are the women waging struggles all over the world?!

Himani: Precisely. Then they tell me that these women, these "immigrant" women don't understand how to fight. I went to a meeting a couple of weeks ago where a woman from Vietnam came, and the questions they asked her were really amazing. This woman headed a huge army unit of missile operators, and they were trying to teach her about non-traditional occupations! (*Makeda and Dionne laugh*)

This woman was with a group of thirty-five women - a detachment on top of a cliff. They had six American destroyers to their credit. These women lived on top of trees - in tree houses - and operated missiles and they are telling them about how to be non-traditional?!

Dionne: That also happened at a meeting Makeda and I went to. There was a woman from Zimbabwe, from a women's co-op there - a group of women who grow their own food and farm. They were a part of the fighting. So here we were at the meeting, and they were asking her things like, "Well, what do the men do?" These women have fought!

Makeda: And then a white woman got up and said to her, "If women can do the same work as men, how come they are not equal?"

Dionne: A lot of women who come to hear these women are sort of backward. I think that sometimes the women from Third World countries who come here to speak decide not to answer some questions because they are so absurd. Then, of course the white women in the audience think, "Oh, they don't know any better." But the woman is probably saying to herself, "What the hell is this? Give me the money and let me go home." (*laughter*)

Himani: The presumptions are really quite interesting. They asked the Vietnamese woman what she did after the war. So she said "We hadn't seen our children for a long time. We went home; we wanted to be with our children, our husbands, our families." And then she was asked, "Well, what have you learned from the revolution? It seems you are still dependent on the children." She said "Children are very important for us, most of our children are dying and there's a lot of damage because of napalm." But since they entirely identified her concern for children with a tight little gender role - without seeing that the child is a symbol in the Third World not just of motherhood in an oppressive sense - they refuse to understand her. They refuse to understand that people have carried on a struggle for twenty-five years against the most powerful armed enemy in the world and won it. Then they try to say that these women are still backward, traditional and unenlightened about the role of men and women in society. What the hell is going on? To believe that these women who fought so hard will not fight anymore, that they are little dolls .... It isn't that we don't have patriarchy or sexism. But what really struck me was the audacity of standing in front of a woman in her mid-forties who had fought twenty-five years in trenches and telling her that *she* doesn't understand what it means to have a non-traditional occupation.

Two Poems by **Clarita Roja**

To a Woman Provincemate

This is not the face I have known
Unlined, unbroken full and glowing
Broken eyes seeing beyond
And beyond seeing.

Oh how the clarity has gone
But how I love you still.

Beloved provinciana.
What is it the big city has made of you
Attuned now to the rat race
Dog poised to eat fellow dog?

You are worried, you say,
About the eyebags, the glamour lost
And yet are glad about the hardening,
The learning of gut logic.

Oh how the clarity has gone
But how I love you still

When the heart hardens
The face hardens with it;
The bones stick out, poised to strike...
And that is how beauty is wasted.

But how I love you still

Come home to the wild,
Uncivilized world,
Most beloved,
Though I may lose you, come home.

The hardening of the heart
Is only for competitors in trade;
Champions of oppressed classes
Have only

Unlined, unbroken full and glowing
Brown eyes seeing beyond
And beyond seeing. Come home.
Join us in the mountain wilds

And though I may lose you
I shall love you deeper still.

Are You My Mother?

Are you my mother?
We have not much in common.
You strut around
Boasting of the riches of your sons and daughters,
Priding yourself in their careers.
Your world is of marble and parquet floors
Polished and scrubbed day after day
By a retinue of meekened maids.
And the cushions
The thick abominable cushions,
That slitheringly whisper your treacherous language of
Surrender, surrender to the heathen god.

You are not my mother.
My vision is not your vision.
My lingo is not of creams that banish scars
But of scars that banish bourgeois dreams.
My mother is she
Who waits in a hut by the hills
With a cup of her *malunggay* soup
And urges me always to
Fight on, daughter, fight on.
The hills are filled with huts
Inside of which are mothers
And so everywhere I go
The atmosphere reverberates with the warmth
Of soup and revolutionary understanding.
And always, the eternal echoing call:
FIGHT ON, DAUGHTER, FIGHT ON!

Towards a "Weapon of Theory" for Black and Working Class Women's Liberation

Cecilia Green

A review of *Women, Race and Class* by Angela Y. Davis.
New York: Random House, 1981.

It is becoming increasingly apparent that white upper-and middle-class North American women can fight for and partially win their "liberation" from patriarchal oppressiveness, leaving the "innermost secret" of capitalism - relations of production/exploitation based on race/nationality and class - untouched.

This does not mean that women's liberation is not "relevant" to non-white and working class women, nor does it mean that middle class women do not suffer sexist oppression, even in fundamental ways. In fact, it should be clear that a focal undertaking of revolutionary politics has always been to establish the terms and conditions of a *necessary* alliance, whose bottom line is the defence and advance of *working class interests*, between the working class and middle class groups and individuals, some of whom serve the revolutionary movement, as we well know, in critical leadership capacities. It is also clear that mass campaigns around specific "women-related" concerns such as suffrage, birth control, abortion, equal rights amendments, rape laws and daycare have brought and could bring together women of all classes and races, in however limited a way. Furthermore, individual middle class women have, especially during the long period marking the formation of the welfare state in Britain and North America, played crucial pioneering roles in the struggles of their working class sisters for various forms and welfare, birth control, housing, protective legislation, unionization. These hardy reformers often saw their constituencies as precisely working class women, families and communities, and often played their roles with courage and proselytizing zeal.

Our opening statement does, however, mean that mass campaigns around issues of critical concern to all oppressed women can and have all too often come to be interpreted, socially constructed and indeed appropriated by exclusivist white middle class interests within those versions which claim media, government and academic attention and which can be accommodated within related hegemonic structures. As Angela Davis has definitively demonstrated in the book I am about to review, issues like abortion can hold different meanings for women of different classes and can occupy different locations within the total repertoire of class experiences and interests of these different women.

It also means of course that reformist middle class leadership of working class women's struggles can give way to a tendency to distort the direction and objectives of such struggles, as history has shown. Thirdly, it means that through the medium of an "autonomous women's movement" an increasingly sophisticated and aggressive theory and praxis of feminism can come to predominate which refuse to treat class and race as issues *central* to its paradigm and which mark the widening of the gap (objective and subjective) between white middle class women and working class women of all colours. This ongoing fine tuning of feminist existentialism and its concomitant praxis have reached a point where those who attempt to re-introduce the centrality of race/nationality and class (to the question of capitalist patriarchy) are dismissed with convenient cliches and not-so-cliches: they are seen as nationalists, imbued with false consciousness, guilty of simplistic analysis, male-dominated left "politicos" etc, etc. Nonetheless, those of us who are painfully cognizant of the skeletons of working class defeats strewn over the battlefields of history do not need to be convinced that upper- and middle-class women's struggles against intra-class sexism do not necessarily attack except tangentially in some cases, the roots of racist and classist patriarchy, whose most exploited and oppressed victims in North America are working class women of colour.

...white women's organizations which fail to incorporate a frontal attack on the racist and class base of U.S. society inevitably become racist and elitist themselves...

There is a further ironic twist to this, the implications of which Angela Davis explores for Afro-American men: non-white working class men are often particularly maligned for their alleged brutishness and sexism. Thus these men who are surely bound to be organizationally and socially beyond the pale of the white middle class feminist encounter (especially if their own organizations do not unequivocally take up the struggle against women's oppression) stand doubly damned: they are seen as the *rapists* and as *ignorant* oppressors. Some white middle class men in whose interest it is to adopt as quickly as possible the accoutrements of non-sexist language and styles are getting all the badges forthcoming, to denote their individual triumph over the disease of sexism and the rapid disappearance of all its traces from their constitutions. Once again, the victims are seen as the perpetrators of society's problems. The crime of rape, after all, is hardly readily associated with "respectable" white upper- and middle-class men. Sexism among working class men, which is undoubtedly a huge problem, and semi-official and official, institutionalized male supremacy both get obfuscated.

Angela Davis' book *Women, Race and Class* could not have appeared at a better time. While it deals specifically with the U.S., there are important lessons to be drawn by Canadians.

Toronto's relatively new non-white immigrant communities are having to deal with increasingly horrible social, psychological and economic pressures at the same time as they are having to get these problems politically recognized and articulated and distinguish between authentic and inauthentic extra-community allies. While there are definitely some genuine alliances, the *problems* Third World immigrant women in particular encounter with white feminist groups come in three forms: (1) a push to popularize "women's struggles" which do not incorporate an address to the special class oppression of immigrant and working class women; (2) a strategy pursued by some groups of cynically demonstrating that they are fulfilling the requisites of a multi-ethnic feminism by forming spurious and token alliances with "ethnic" women who bear no politically significant relationship to "their" ethnic communities; (3) the attempt by some "feminists" (who rather amazingly manage to maintain their credibility with their less aggressive counterparts) to make a career out of "taking over" immigrant women's struggles, ostensibly with the noble aim of injecting them with the "correct" feminist theory.

Recent struggles within organizations serving immigrant women in Toronto cogently bore out these concerns. These struggles also taught the following lesson: that the immigrant/working class women's movement (broadly conceived) in Toronto urgently needs to articulate a theory - of its constituencies, their oppression and its struggle. It needs the "weapon of theory," both as a ready critique of ethnocentric and petty bourgeois feminism, and most important-ly, as a means of clearly and decisively advancing its own interests and shaping the struggle for women's liberation. This theory is of course partially embedded in the ideas and experiences of, for example, the Toronto activists who recently rose to defend the control of organizations for immigrant women by representative immigrant women and their allies. However it needs to be pulled together, deepened and articulated.

Enter Angela Davis.

In a way the United States provides a particularly legible and useful context for the exploration of the issues just raised. It has a relatively long tradition of movements of middle class white women who have had to deal every step of the way with the intractable presence of a huge American-born-and-bred subordinated non-white population. This history is a source of widely applicable insights and lessons.

Davis powerfully establishes the two conclusions reached through the unfolding of that history: white women's organizations which fail to incorporate in their analyses and praxes a frontal attack on the racist and class base of U.S. society inevitably become racist and elitist themselves, less and less by default and more and more by intention. Secondly, an examination of the historical and struc-tural location of Afro-American women within U.S. society holds the key to the inner chambers of its racist male supremacy. As a corollary of this, Davis documents the militant resistance with which Black women have met their oppression all along the way, a story that has often been deliberately down-played or hidden, even by feminist historians. Indeed, to date, in spite of the recent proliferation of writing on the history of the women's rights move-ment in the U.S., one of the most honest and inclusive accounts remains Eleanor Flexner's *Century of Struggle*,[1] first published in 1959! Davis pays homage to that work as she does to all the fearless white women who risked incurring the terrible wrath of their society by their refusal to compromise on the discomfiting questions of race and class. Two of the pioneers among white women to combine a struggle against racism, sexism and class exploitation, whom Davis singles out for special attention, are the Grimké sisters, Sarah and Angelina, the famous anti-slavery agitators.

Davis begins her account with slavery. She takes "the starting point for any exploration of Black women's lives under slavery" to be "an appraisal of their role as workers" (p.5). Thus, in the nineteenth century, while many white women were labouring under the burden of a new "ideology of femininity" which legitimated the transfer of the productive centre from the home to the factory by inflating and glorifying the attenuated domestic and sex-roles of (house-) wife and mother, Black women were fulfilling the unequivocal functions of worker (mostly in the field), breeder (of slave infant property) and sex object (of their white masters).

The forced incompatibility between the slave woman's role of worker and "breeder" on the one hand and mother on the other was starkly symbolized by the painfully swollen breasts of newly confined mothers working in the field and the grief-stricken cries of mothers whose children were being sold away from them. It was also symbolized by the rebellious response of some slave women who chose abortion over giving life to children destined for slavery, or infanticide over letting them endure it. Such defiant acts and the disguised form of rape that Black women had to constantly endure at the hands of their masters were perversely inverted against their already beleaguered selves through such myths as their strange and inhuman lack of a "maternal instinct" and their "natural" immorality.

Thus "Black women enjoyed few of the dubious benefits of the ideology of womanhood" (p.5), and if they were "hardly 'women' in the accepted sense, the slave system also discouraged male supremacy in Black men" (p.7).

According to Davis (and most writers on the subject), the slave relation of production practically obliterated gender and made for a minimal sexual division of labour, since slave men and women performed essentially the same tasks in the field. (In addition, she de-mythologizes the "Black Mammy" figure of the house-servant). But while the system of slavery imposed a "terrible burden of equality in oppression" (p.19) on Black women, Davis sees this "negative equality" being transformed on another level into a positive force: both in terms of the pride Black women were able to attain in their work, also a source of confidence and identity for them, and in terms of the "egalitarianism characterizing their social-relations" (p.18) in the domestic sphere (i.e., with their men).

Davis' thesis, that through their work roles and by escaping "the dubious benefits of the ideology of womanhood" slave women were ironically able to achieve relatively healthy self-identities and rela-tions with men, has been supported by writers of many different stripes and contains an extremely important truth. However, there are some problems. By arguing along a single path, Davis effectively steers clear of the more nuanced controversies and contradictions, embedded in the more easily resolved ones. Obviously her analysis provides a clear refutation of the "Black Matriarchy" Moynihan thesis: firstly, Black women are among the most exploited victims of a racist patriarchy, and secondly, a degree of sexual equality within the Black community has been both a historical necessity and evidence of health and strength rather than social pathology. Davis also implicitly provides a challenge to grossly overrated theories about "Black Macho" such as those spread by Michele Wallace in her viciously distorted little book *Black Macho and the Myth of the Superwoman*,[2] much loved by some white feminists, even if its author indiscriminately maligns Black woman *and* white women along with Black men! (For white men she seems to reserve either an ambiguous admiration or silence. Wallace herself is Black).

But many questions remain. Why does Davis neglect to throw light on the shaping of the structure of sexism among Black working class men? If we agree that every clearly demarcated social formation under capitalism is imbued with its own "pathological" potential (emanating *partially* from the structure of its exploitation), what is the "pathology" of male-female relations in the Afro-American sub-culture? Is Black male sexism a post-emancipation phenomenon then? And if this so-called pathology is merely a received reflection of prevailing and dominant mores in the wider society (as some argue), what, anyhow, is the Black community's version of male supremacy? If Davis wants to talk to Black women she cannot simply make these questions out to be tangential ones.

There is also a question about the uses Davis makes of writers like Eugene Genovese and Herbert Gutman. These writers, having un-dertaken the somewhat dubiously conceived task of restoring the beleaguered "dignity" of Afro-Americans by means of a re-writing of their history, seem at pains to point out either that Blacks made fantastic and heroic slaves (Genovese, *Roll, Jordan, Roll*)[3] or that

The Seneca Falls Declaration did not address the situation of slave and free Black women or of white working class women.

against all odds their yearnings and behaviour patterns were indistinguishable from those of whites (Gutman, *The Black Family in Slavery and Freedom*)[4]. While Davis is cognizant of these problems, she does not sufficiently question Gutman's thesis that the slaves and freedmen magnificently achieved, wherever they could and within the limits imposed upon them, "stable" two parent families complete with the "appropriate" sex roles.

By this argument and the one that the female-headed Black family is to be more precisely understood as a modern phenomenon, Gutman, supposedly well-intentionedly, hopes to quelch the "disorganization" thesis. But many Blacks are suspicious of what they see as a glorificationist trend among white chroniclers of the Afro-American experience, even the well-meaning ones. Nathan Hare has a point when he warns us to beware those who would deny the terrible ravages that Black family relations have suffered through a romantic and even celebrationist rendering of their reality.[5] While it is not clear whether Hare is lamenting the "loss" of patriarchy as some Black male scholars do (I did not get the feeling that he was), we cannot easily ignore this aspect of things and its attendant problems. Finally, of course, as Davis herself notes, both Gutman and Genovese assume the superiority and desirability of white cultural norms (sex roles) and impute to Black people behaviourial patterns premised on these. At least one other writer has gone further than Davis and questioned Gutman's quite explicit refusal to consider the slaves' adherence to their own reconstituted African norms and his tendency to "read off" European patterns from the behaviour of the slaves.[6] Also, quite apart from the question of cultural origins, one remains curious about the sexual- and class-political implications of "stable" slave families. All in all, it is clear that while Davis has managed a stunning breakthrough, she has not adequately brought together the questions of culture, "deviance" and the intransigent effects of exploitation in relation to Black woman's triumphs *and* tears.

Most of the first half of the book is actually taken up with a discussion of the roots and development of the women's rights movement in the U.S.; however, I consider the opening chapter which takes up the above issues to be of crucial importance.

According to Davis "(t)he inestimable importance of the Seneca Falls Declaration was its role as the *articulated consciousness of women's rights* at midcentury." (p.53). Nonetheless, it "proposed an analysis of the female condition which disregarded the circumstances of women outside the social class of the document's framers." (p.54). Davis examines the politicized transposition of white women's energies, in their own interests, from the abolition movement to the women's rights movement in nineteenth century America. Male supremacy within the anti-slavery movement, especially grating in view of the hard work done by the female participants, together with the transfer of production out of the home, leaving it a glorified prison for the new well-to-do "housewife," often educated and with a lot of time on her hands, contrived to bring home sharply to these women the contradictions of their existence. The Seneca Falls Declaration, a pioneering attempt to systematically articulate their grievances and demands, was therefore a "rigorous consummation of the consciousness of white middle-class women's dilemma" (p.53). It did not address the situation of slave and free Black women or of white working class women, especially the "mill girls" of the Northeast.

The eventual concession of the women's rights movement to explicitly racist arguments and principles has been documented by writers other than Davis. Angelina Grimké had from very early on criticized the racism of the women's anti-slavery societies and herself embodied a radical rejection of that racism. The circumstances of Sojourner Truth's famous 1851 "Ain't I a Woman" speech is now well known. Davis reminds us that the women who formed the early suffrage movement had graduated from an Abolition Movement which was not in the least opposed to Northern capitalism or in favour of workers' rights. In relation to the slaves the movement did not see and was not interested in looking beyond the single act of emancipation, considering it, and that *explicitly*, to be all that was needed to correct the wrongs of slavery. Frederick Douglass and William Lloyd Garrison had fought over this position.

Davis skilfully urges us to look at the famous and unfortunate debate of votes for the Negro (men) versus votes for (white) women in that light as well as in the context of the reign of terror which had been unleashed on Black people in the South by their former masters. Of course the debate should never have taken place: its

Margaret Sanger...moved...to an alliance...with those who openly advocated the racist strategy of poulation control

terms were imposed by the exigencies of the situation and the restrictive parameters of the capitalist legislative process. However, the issue of the *investiture of "the Negro"* (unfortunately through the male, according to patriarchal capitalist law) *with common citizenship in American society*, at a time when men and women were at the daily mercy of the lynch mob and the subject of constant schemes (government and otherwise) for mass deportation to foreign lands, stood by itself as an absolute priority. Although Davis points to the limitations of the vote per se and criticizes Douglass for his exaggerated and naive belief in its range of possibilities, I still think its importance should not be underestimated, especially when looked at in conjunction with other demands that the "Black Liberation Movement" was making at the time.

The fact that the debate was shaped into a bitter contest was also directly attributable to the white supremacist foundations of the arguments used by the women's suffrage movement to advance their own cause. From arguing no votes for the Negro without the vote for women, especially since they had held their (middle class) suffrage demands in abeyance during the Civil War, they regressed to votes for intelligent and civilized white women *instead of* votes for ignorant and brutish Black and immigrant men. Votes for white women would save the race ... and with that they struck up an alliance with those Southern white interests who were intent on brutalizing Black people back into a second form of slavery. At the 1903 convention of National American Woman Suffrage Association (NAWSA), Belle Kearney from Mississippi could say with impunity: "The enfranchisement of women would insure immediate and durable white supremacy, honestly attained..." (p. 125). And this, as Davis notes, from the organized white women's movement at a time when capitalism was evolving its most advanced and most terroristic ideological and economic apparatus of racism.

Davis documents much the same story for other movements, notably, later on in the book, the early birth control movement led by Margaret Sanger who moved from Socialist party membership in 1912 to an alliance years later with those who openly advocated the racist strategy of population control in order to save the "superior" race from the "inferior." In addition she notes the organized white women's years of silence and stalling on the question of lynching at a time when Black women were leading the fight against it, their racism towards Black members and Black sister groups of the Club Movement, and their lack of protest when Black women were forcibly prevented from exercising their newly won right to vote.

On the positive side she documents Black women's own efforts at organization - against slavery, for suffrage, against lynching. The latter struggle occupied the militant energies of two outstanding Black female leaders, Mary Church Terrell and Ida B. Wells, and scored impressive successes. Davis briefly explores the needs and struggles of white working women as well and their relationship to the causes of abolition and suffrage, which did not occupy centre stage in their lives until a powerful argument could be raised linking the need for suffrage to the struggle against class exploitation. Finally, on the positive side, Davis celebrates the unprecedented and unsurpassed solidarity achieved between fighting Black and white women during the Reconstruction campaigns to educate the freedmen.

The rest of the book, from chapter ten onwards, does not follow the highlighted historical progression traced up to then, but constitutes a series of related essays, on "Communist Women," "Rape, Racism and the Myth of the Black Rapist." "Racism, Birth Control and Reproductive Rights" and "The Approaching Obsolescence of Housework: A Working-Class Perspective." Of these by far the most powerful and most important is the one on rape and racism.

The chapter on Communist women constitutes a clearly inadequate substitute for an analysis that Davis seems not to be bothered to undertake. Why Communism? This question does not raise an objection to Communism but to the fact that the question never gets asked. If Davis' book is meant to be a grassroots account for a grassroots audience then it is seriously presumptuous in its leap from a careful presentation of the documented historical factors to the miraculously conjured up Communist requisite. Communism is conveniently *asserted* as non-problematic, both on the woman question and on the Black question presumably. If Communism as a concrete movement with a *concrete* history in the U.S. is the answer, then surely Davis owes it to her fully intelligent and anxious grass roots readership to provide *concrete* (and theoretical of course) proof beyond mere sketches of individual and undoubtedly heroic Communist women? Davis has left us at the stage where Black women are mostly domestic and service workers. How did the not-exactly-harmonious relationship between Northern white industrial labour and Southern Black non-industrial labour become resolved? What happened when Black labour went North? What was the role of Communist organisations in all these processes? How does the Communist Party of which Davis is a member pull together the questions of class, race and gender? What is its relationship to Blacks? To women? To Black women?

The questions are not hostile ones. Black women in particular will want to know for sure, and are willing to learn. It is a pity Davis has chosen not to explain.

Davis' final chapter is also a bit weak. One is disappointed that she has not chosen to tackle the all important question of Black women and welfare frontally and to provide us with her characteristically militant and incisive insights. Again, Davis seems not to be connecting quite as directly as in the first two thirds of her book to the demanding reality of Black women's lives and the need for a working class Black woman's perspective. She focuses almost entirely on a critique of white feminist theories and practices. But her critique of the "Wages for Housework" group is not particularly powerful (which is unfortunate for Toronto readers) and her call for the socialization of housework somewhat abstract and question-begging. This criticism is not as true of her solid contextuation of the abortion debate and her prioritization of a call for an end to sterilization abuse.

The chapter on rape, though brilliant, is problematic in ways with which one has grown familiar by this stage of her book, Davis neatly reverses Shulamith Firestone's absurd thesis that racism is an extension of sexism by arguing that rape, the most brutal weapon of sexism, is an extension of racism. Davis views rape from the point of view of an act of violence essentially governed by racist class relations between white men and Black women. She also attacks the crude assumptions by some white feminists on rape that Black men are particularly prone to the latter (through no fault of their own of course...) as a racist concession to the hundreds of hysterical, false charges of rape that became a weapon of legitimation in the hands of the Southern lynch mob. She raises the all important issues of the discrepancy between reported and unreported rape, the association of "police blotter" with rapists in general and the class and racist bias of rape prosecution.

It is true that rape by white men of Black women, especially when called by another name and justified by the alleged "looseness" of Black women, has been historically a fundamental building block and index of capitalist America's racist patriarchy. It has borne the distinction of being officially or semi-officially sanctioned by the racist order. Furthermore, *Black men too are victims of that racist patriarchy*, as manifested by the false rape charges of the lynching era and the negative discrimination against them (i.e., in relation to white rapists) in the system of arrest and prosecution for rape. In fact, Davis shows that, *in sharp contrast to the prosecution of Black rapists*, only three white men were tried, convicted and executed for lynching between 1865 and 1895, during which period more that 10,000 Black people were murdered in cold blood (p. 184).

Davis' analysis is an absolutely crucial intervention into the still blurry debate on rape. It is in the immediate interest of Black people in particular to find out the truth about rape, and Davis certainly clears away a lot of the cobwebs. However, she does not sufficiently highlight the distinction between rape as an expression of class exploitation and rape as an intra-class and intra-ethnic (not to speak of domestic) phenomenon. Rape, after all, has a relatively autonomous *sexist* existence, and as such Black women bear a double burden - racist rape and intra-ethnic "sexist" rape. When a Black woman is being raped by a Black man it is small comfort to her that rape by white men has been an historic weapon in the construction of a racist patriarchy or that Black men have been historic victims of malicious false rape charges. Davis offers little insight into that problem.

On the whole, Davis' book stands as a principled if uncompromising account of the meeting place of women, race and class. Ironically, while one or two self-styled Black feminists have denounced the racism of the American white women's movement in particularly cynical (a-historical and a-theoretical) ways, Davis, who probably would not call herself a Black feminist without some qualification, does so in a far more *principled* and *concrete* manner. She does not allow spurious fads to lead her to compromise her scientific assessment of such historical figures as Frederick Douglass, a Black man, or Angelina Grimké, a white woman, both of whom she establishes as firm allies of the Black and working class women's struggle for liberation. If the unorganized Black working class women's voice sometimes appears to be muted or lack spontaneity in her book, Davis has nonetheless given us an indispensable lesson in how to listen to that voice and what to listen for when it speaks its oppression and attempts to resist it. For sure, for those of us who know the bottom line, we shall be able to detect when that voice is missing entirely, even amidst the most strident mouthing of cries for "liberation."

NOTES

1. Eleanor Flexner, *A Century of Struggle: The Woman's Rights Movement in the United States*. Massachusetts: Belknap Press of Harvard University Press, 1959.

2. Michele Wallace, *Black Macho and the Myth of the Superwoman*. New York: Dial Press, 1979.

3. Eugene Genovese, *Roll, Jordan, Roll: The World the Slaves Made*. New York: Pantheon Books, 1974. Genovese also seems to be arguing that the white Southern planters made fantastic and heroic masters.

4. Herbert Gutman, *The Black Family in Slavery and Freedom, 1750-1925*. New York: Pantheon Books, 1976. Gutman's thesis has more grassroots and radical appeal than Genovese's.

5. Nathan Hare, "Revolution Without a Revolution: The Psychosociology of Sex and Race," *The Black Scholar*, Vol. 9, No. 7 (April 1978), pp. 2-7.

6. Niara Sudarkasa, "African and Afro-American Family Structure: A Comparison", *The Black Scholar*, Vol. 11, No. 8 (Nov./Dec. 1980), pp. 37-60.

Kerri Sakamoto

She felt content to admire him from afar. He was so utterly different from her. They were like two crookedly parallel lines; the space between would always be great, but never could they become oblique. She was accustomed to feeling distanced from the rest of the world. In everyday life she would seem to be a part of things; she had many friends but she never told them how far away from them she felt, watching their pink faces and hearing the sound of her own high, thin voice, seeing her hand, yellow skin taut across it wave before her face, or seeing a strand of black hair fall over her eye. She hated mirrors in public washrooms; they only made the disparity too brittley apparent. He was ever further removed from her circle of friends. He was only to be seen from a vast distance like an objet d'art.

She saw him long before he saw her - long before she even believed that he might see her. She would watch him striding purposefully past her in the university library where she sat in her usual place off to the side of the aisle. It seemed to her that she was always seeing him in passing, and his scent, travelling less quickly behind

him, would nimbly whirl over her, crisp and clean. She watched after him and what she noticed was the way his cleanly cut hair around the nape of his neck bristled against the upturned collar of his overcoat. The overcoat was dark in colour, so dark that she could never discern whether it was black or blue. But the colour didn't matter because the coat itself gave him something when he put it on and tucked up the collar to his white neck, his smooth cheek. It gave his silhouette strength and definition. His eyes seemed larger and of a clearer, unclouded brown. She often saw him drape it casually on his chair in the cafeteria, its bottom edge falling upon the floor. She wondered at the ill treatment of this beautiful coat that transformed him so, at the potency held within its dark, dense folds. One day, she stood near him as he strode past her and let her hand brush gently against its cloth. The sensation sighed gently on her hand for a moment before fleeing. She stood for a time after he had gone. He never saw her, never felt her hand upon his sleeve; his eyes only saw what was in his path.

She began watching him closely, learning where he would be at certain times on certain days, watching him in conversation swing his head to one side and his hair swish across his forehead. She loved his way of simply forgetting himself - something which she could never do. He would walk directly to the shelf in the library where the book he sought lay and upon finding it, a richly boyish "ah," would slip out into the heaviness of the room. She loved his positive, striding aura never impeded by his own self, never seeming to falter or to linger an instant too long. But one day in the library, he faltered; his eyes wavered then looked strangely through the distance at her. It was so unexpected; it felt like a violation of her private space. She was afraid and quickly lowered her eyes. When she looked up several moments later, he was gone.

It was in the library that he first noticed her. She had tucked herself away in a quiet corner and he never would have seen her had the book he needed not been on the shelf opposite the table at which she was seated. He was reminded of a Japanese mural he had once seen in a gallery. The sight of her brought back to him the serene figure of a woman softly enfolded in a kimono of dove grey with blushing pink flowers. Her face was drawn with tender yielding strokes of a brush. That was how he saw this girl in the library. He was continually intrigued by the uplifted outer corners of her eyes, the simple blackness of her hair, the golden yellow of her skin. He saw her pitter with tiny, apologetic steps around and between large volumes of encyclopedias and dictionaries as she would around and between bodies in the crowded cafeteria. He felt he would overwhelm her with his own size and weight. Her head usually faced the ground as she walked and her eyes strained widely upward to compensate for her head's downward tilt. As she spoke, her slender arms formed the fragile branches of a symbolic Oriental flower arrangement evoking the positions of heaven and earth. And her hand gesturing delicately with open palms blossomed forth femininity and vulnerability. They caressed the air and floated down through it in gentle harmony with gravity. In nodding her head, it was with an arc-like movement, never with a straight line, as if she were dulling the hard absoluteness of an emphatic yes or no. When he heard her speak for the first time, it seemed to him that she had polished all the edges of the words which softly slipped from between her lips until each phrase was a rippling undulation. Her smile, very sweetly contained, was a perfect cadence. Once she discovered his observation of her and he felt suddenly very aware of himself, very awkward as he never did before. He tried to smile but his lips hesitated and she turned her eyes away from him. He quickly left the library feeling exposed and vulnerable.

He finally introduced himself. It was in the cafeteria at lunchtime. She was sitting alone, her face partially eclipsed by the sandwich she was holding. He said hello and sat down opposite her, stumbling at the vision of her face so close to his. She feared her silent nervousness being revealed and he feared his tumbling words sounding too glibly high-pitched. Later they began to walk together. She had to scurry with his strides. Perched on his arm, she saw the ground hurry beneath them, all the while watching his straight encompassing steps beside her small, straining ones. Her hand slipped into the side pocket of his coat, her palm luxuriating in the satin folds of its lining.

He bought her many things, among them a small Oriental doll with a white porcelain face and a brightly coloured kimono enclosed in a glass case. She loved it because he had given it to her. They both loved to gaze at its untouchable loveliness. They had begun to know one another well yet they each still felt a certain unease with their disparity. She would turn away from their reflection in shop windows and she snipped herself out of a photograph which had captured the two of them side by side. He said nothing when he saw it.

One night as they lay together on his bed, she enfolded in his coat and his arms, the telephone rang. The sound was startling at first then seemed to grow louder and more insistent with each ring. He rose hesitantly to answer it in the hallway and began to speak in a quiet voice. She heard a name, a name that seemed too familiar on his lips. It brought to mind a face she had seen whose contours she remembered as fitting well with his. She still waited wrapped in his coat which suddenly was repulsive to her. She cast it away from her, hearing in her mind again the shrill voice of the ringing telephone that drowned out the sound of any words that they might ever have uttered to one another and that abruptly interrupted the passage of his sweet scent and matted the smooth nap of his magnificent coat. His voice grew quiet again then stopped remembering her in the next room. They both heard the receiver drop into place. They endured a moment of heavy silence in separate rooms. He walked slowly back into the room looking the calm, the sure. She felt sudden angry streaks across her face. Not her voice, not her hands, not her words flying up sharp and wild into the air rampantly tearing into boyish flesh. Where was the self so long, so carefully nurtured? He no longer knew her. He left her standing spent, wondering at herself, at the closed door, at the emptiness of the room, scentless and still. His coat lay sprawled across the floor where she had flung it. She noticed that it was blue.

Three Poems by **Claire Harris**

I brood on the uselessness of letters

Tu Fu 713-770

The moon like a wandering period punctuates my dismal
night thoughts   between the trees at the foot of the alley
the city glitters in the river   its drowned life made
mysterious by ripples...   in this deep I am an enchantress
in a cave of echoing ancient prophecies   my hair weeds in
tides that erode the town at the rivers edge   I cast words
like bones read the mysteries of earth and sky for petitioners
whose drowned eyes like pebbles washed by the stream
cannot close   before my revelations they shake tremulous
to plead.....   Helpless before bombs that melt flesh
the   technical miracle of phosphorus clarified by
newscasts I cannot write winds shiver in the trees   the
laughter of women, the clink of glasses rise from the terrace
below my window   I toss and turn on the pillows   long
for the safety of words and images

Noon and the August haze veils the gentle eastern hills the
prim modest houses   along the Bow the poplars grow
yellow   stranded on the deck of this ship perched on the
cliffs edge I watch the steel city flaring in the high noon so
bright I must look away   here where no one walks the
traffic strung out at the lights like the coils of a python
tightens around the city endlessly   in the median men on
huge earth movers go busily about their work   cocooned
in their own noise CP air drones through the pale blue   I
imagine the passengers settling back before the long
suspension   and home   So distant from my own
rainforested mountains   mountains rounded like whales
stranded against the dawn   light lapping their ridges the
tiny shacks like barnacles riding their flanks   palms burst
into green spume against the sky   I remember the dark
faces streaming out of the valleys   black women flowing
currents & waves   their feet solid on the earth their
unreasoned unhurried grace   this forever and indelible
on the inner eye   This summer shades into the sixteenth
autumn   I grow yellow in exile

the open ones carry/the stone behind the eyes/it recognises you
Celan/Felistiner

Once it must have been
possible to think
that no one waking
in the moonlight says
one day I will play
football   a baby
as the ball   but this
is recorded
a doctor cracking
the skull of a boy
writes down the date
how long it takes
to heal   then cracks
the skull again and
writes the date   a man
of culture and science
the boy cracked to
death   I would like to
it must once have been
possible   now it
is recorded
they buried the small
boy alive lest he
grow to take up arms
and bombs were tested
that splintered & flamed
in the flesh   for days
and there was rejoicing
at our success

\- 1 -

That day was born red & dusty
from the old man's tales   his
grandfather
plaiting the intricate mats   the
muttering day thick in his mouth
of rifle butts and skulls   how
the sun goes down in the heart
how quickly the watchful air cools
how dangerously after the hot work
that day   an old man's spittling
memories of cool blue mountain
mornings
of peasants and soldiers

54

- 2 -

At dawn the sardonic sun dragged him out of arms   Rosa watching
him   her eyes like the eyes of her small daughters who never spoke in
his presence   now whispering from the verandah mat   eyes as if
they judged the pesos he left could buy only pestilence   A morning
like any other   except for the new rifle   the feel of it in his hands
the power surge of bullets sprayed like piss the knowledge like a song
if there was no ambush he would get home alive even if there was his
luck would hold   this to be his last day in the mountains   The sun
reached his eyes and his smile which was for his son Tomasito who
jumped up & down at the gate squealing with delight at the miracle of
his arrival   and it was for Maria smiling her special secret smile but
asking nothing

Even his smile included the old man in the banana shade near the hedge
the dreaming truck clattered to a stop   And   the orders given to
punishment   he crossed himself secretly   still he did not know

not very long ago
in Tasmania
men   and women (?)
dressed in scarlet
to hunt the natives
I see them civil   in hounds & horn
new comers blooded
with ceremony
they come home to tea
today   unwilling
to risk the eyes we
kill   over Winnipeg
clouds of disease
deliberately
to find how much is
enough
there must have been
a morning
once   a flash in time
when it seemed
we understood
but today we spend
ourselves
in the pure research of
mega death
the planet destroyed
if necessary
life   for the supremacy
of an economic
theory

- 3 -

So it was
he went down
the red & dusty road
passed fields fading & brittle in the light
passed the burnt-out trucks
without premonition   even
in the closed villages   the woman was
waiting for him on the stoop   unyielding
contempt slanting in her eyes
the bundle casual in her arms   those
eyes a sudden swamp in his path
the blood boiling   her eyes were
a swamp that rose up & swallowed him

- 4 -

In her arms the bundle stirred & cried her face gentled   he saw her
soft as a breeze   then she looked at him   a surge of envy/rage such
that he moved towards her without volition jumped from the moving
truck towards her   and she startled back as he reached out &
grabbed at the child   held on   would not yield   he swung the
riflebutt   she   staggered   her eyes open there rose waterlogged
from those depths the root & branches of hate trapped & drowning he

shouted "ojos malos"   she lunged forward   And he threw the baby
to Gonzales who laughing caught it as expertly as he once caught balls
in the Square   juggled with one hand & tossed the bundle over his
head to another the   wrappings flailing   in the laughter her eyes
closed

release he turned to the game   over the crackle of gunfire the bundle
tossed to him   the air refused it the light bending away out of its
darkness a mouth opening   his boot reached out beyond the woman
her hair falling over her face her bleeding mouth trapped in an O

who read this
"Stricken by
and seeking reality[2]"
know
we die
piece by piece
for this greed
we fashion
to a species
of grace
We would
like   need
to believe

- 5 -

no one
wakes

and the softness   *at dawn*
softer than he had expected   *saying*
he saw the spreading stain   *today*
as he hit the ground behind the truck   *if necessary*
the sun gone down within him   *I will kick*
from the darkness he fired   *a baby*
at the women   the old men   *you*
the boys coming at him with rakes   *to death   you*
with machetes   and curses   *would like to*
with ancient guns   *but*
with sticks that broke   *it may never*
                                                        have been possible

[2]*Festiner/Celan - 1958 Speech Bremen Literary prize A.P. R. Vol 11 No. 4*

Indian woman and child along shoreline

The Public Archives of Canada

Profiles of Working Class East Indian Women

Interviewed and Translated by
Prabha Khosla

Two Hundred Pants a Day

Kewal Hundal is forty-eight years old and works in one of the largest clothing manufacturing plants in the Metro Toronto Area. The factory employs about five hundred workers. They work in one shift from 8 a.m. to 4.45 p.m.

Ever since I started working here I have been sewing pants. The factory makes men's clothes, specifically, three-piece suits for places such as Tip Top Tailors.

Almost all the workers are women. Although there are all kinds of women working here, I would say the majority are Chinese women. A few men work here, but they primarily work in the area where the material is cut, and I don't know what they are paid.

All the rest of the sewing, cutting and pressing work is done by women. The work is divided into many categories. For example, even though I sew pants, the parts I sew are basically the four seams, two for each leg. Four other women do the same work as me. Two of them are Chinese, one is Black and one is Portuguese. People are not transferred from one part to another very often.

Most of us are paid by the piece. Only a few women, about 10 out of a 100, get an hourly rate. At the hourly rate, you begin at $3.50 an hour and then you get a $0.50 raise every 6 months. There are a few women who make up to $4.50 an hour. But they really make you work on the hourly rate.

I can do 150 to 200 pants a day. I get paid by the piece. So I make $18.00 for every 100 pants. Sometimes, when the material is easier to handle, I can do up to 220 pants a day. Some of the women are really fast, and they can sew 200 to 300 pants a day. So they make more money.

The women who work on the pants are in one area of the factory and those who work on the coats are in another. We are divided into separate sections so that those women who do the buttons are in one area, the ones who sew the zippers in another, and so on. All the work is divided, like an assembly line with different women working on the collars, others sewing the sleeves and the coats, and still others doing the pressing. The clothes have to be ironed during the different stages of sewing, so the pressers are spread out throughout the factory.

There is no uniform wage here. In some areas, the women make more than in others. Like, the women who sew the buttons can make $50.00 to $60.00 a day. But again, they have work really fast, and not waste any time. There is no overtime. Everybody goes home at 4:45 p.m. We get about 45 minutes for lunch.

There used to be another union here and we used to get two fifteen minute breaks. Now we have a different union and we don't get the breaks anymore. As you know, I don't speak English, so I don't always know what is going on. There used to be a young Indian man who talked to me and told me what was happening in the factory, but he doesn't work here anymore. Some of the women seem to prefer to work right through lunch and don't mind if they don't get a break. Others do.

I want to continue working here, because it is so difficult to get another job these days. And anyway, it is better than some of the other work that our people are doing.

Three Children Died Last Year

Most of the farmwork in British Columbia is concentrated in the Fraser and Okanagan Valleys and is done by immigrant workers. In Greater Vancouver, the majority of farmworkers are primarily Indian or Chinese. There is also a small percentage of working class whites. Farmwork is seasonal, and consequently, a large proportion of the workforce is migratory. Some, like the Quebecois workers, travel to the Okanagan Valley every summer to pick fruit. Due to inadequate housing, they usually have to resort to tenting. Many of the farmworkers in the Fraser Valley live a great distance away in the interior of British Columbia. They are accommodated in converted sheds or barns. It is estimated that the majority of the 10,000 farmworkers in British Columbia are girls and women between the ages of 8 to 70 years old. Kuldip Kaur Bains, who is interviewed below is sixty-three years old, a grandmother and a worker.

We come down to this farm about March-April, and we live here the whole summer till the end of August, beginning of September.

This is the third year we have come to this farm: me, my husband, my daughter-in-law and her two children. My son works at the saw mill in Williams Lake. That is where we live. And my daughter-in-law comes later when the children have finished school.

We live in this barn here, that has been converted so that it can now accommodate five families. It's been divided up into five sections, but as you can see, it's all rough work with an unfinished plywood ceiling and the walls are bare gyproc. Nothing has been painted or anything. And there aren't enough light bulbs and there are no windows. We have two bunk beds next to each other with a small table. We keep our clothes and other things under the beds.

In the area outside the bedrooms we have two fridges which we all share and five gas plates - one for each family. The washrooms are outside, around the back and there is no light there either. There are no showers and we wash ourselves by carrying water in buckets. There are two toilets and two small divided areas where we clean ourselves.

We have to make a living, so we just learn to accept these things. It is very difficult for me to get any other work. I'm old and I don't speak English, so this is the only work I can get. We get up early in the morning, make some breakfast, and lunch to take with us to the fields. We don't come back here until the evening.

Avairy Productions

The work is hard and back-breaking. But only us Indians do it. Nobody else will. And we get paid so little. For example, if we pick raspberries we get $2.50 for one flat which weighs 16 1/2lbs. It takes a lot of picking to fill one flat and towards the end of the season it takes even longer. But we don't get the whole $2.50, because the farmer deducts money for allowing us to stay here in his barn. So what we get to keep for ourselves is something like one dollar out of every $2.50.

When we are picking broccoli and cauliflower, we use sharp knives and quite often people get hurt. But there is no first aid on the farm and they usually don't take us to hospital unless it's very serious. So most of us carry bandages with us. Many of us have rashes. People say it's from the pesticides we use on the vegetables and fruits, but the farmer is not doing anything about it.

It's also dangerous for our children. Some of the older children work with their parents but the younger ones stay with their mothers in the field. Three children died last year, because no one was looking after them. They were just playing by themselves.

Because of all these problems, I joined the Canadian Farmworkers Union. They said that if we are all united we will be able to get better money for our work and also be covered by the Worker's Compensation Board. We don't get many of the benefits that other workers get. After all, aren't we like other people? We do the work like everyone else and we should get these things. How would they eat if we were not doing this work?

Is There A Union Here?

Sudha Patel has lived in Canada for eleven years.

One of my first jobs was at this factory that makes things like paper bags and other paper products. We had many different machines to work with. We made big bags for industrial use and the smaller ones like the ones you get at grocery stores. There were only a few Indians in the factory. Actually, I think there were only two or three of us.

The way the factory was set-up was that when we came in in the morning, there was a list on the wall indicating which person was assigned to which machine for that day. The machine would be listed with someone's name next to it. And some of the machines were really fast.

Every morning when I would make my way to the machine with my name, the other women who worked there would always tell me, "No, you can't work at that one. You come and work on this one here." Everytime, they would move me to the fastest one. I had to work really hard and fast. It was so difficult to keep up to the speed of the machine. And I was really tired by the time I got home in the evening. I don't speak English, even though I do understand some, and I never knew who to complain to about the speed of the machine.

So one day I decided that I had had enough of this. I looked at the list and went to the machine which was assigned to me. Again these women told me that I couldn't work on it. But this time I said, "No, the list said that I was to work on this one, so this is where I am going to stay."

Well, because of all the noise and confusion the foreman came over and asked what was going on. After he had assessed the situation he said that I had to work on the other machine and not the one with my name on it. Otherwise I could leave right now. So I left, got my lunch and came home. What was I supposed to do?

The next day I went to apply for unemployment insurance because I didn't know how long it would take me to find another job. But at the U.I.C. office they told me that I couldn't apply for U.I.C. They told me that there was union in the plant and that I shouldn't have walked out, that I should have talked to the union.

I didn't know about the union. I did have a union card, so I guess it's partly my fault. But I didn't know that the union would do anything about it. They never told me about the union and what it was for. Of course, I guess everybody was in the union but nobody did anything about what had been going on for a long time. And I didn't know who I was supposed to talk to.

I do believe in protecting our rights, but if they don't tell us, how are we supposed to know? I didn't even know the name of the union.

Avairy Productions

Avairy Productions

I Want to Learn English

My name is Charanject Dhillon. I was twenty when I came here, five years ago. I had just graduated from the local college in India with a B.A. My first four or five months here, I didn't do anything. I missed home a lot, and used to cry everytime I received letters from my friends. Then, after a while I started realizing that I should get a job, or I should start going to school. So I took English classes. I used to go downtown twice a week to Manpower classes. I took the classes for about three months and then started to look for a job.

I only looked for the jobs that didn't require much English, because I didn't speak enough then. I was looking for work in a restaurant, hotel or motel to do cleaning as a chambermaid. Finally, I found one. It was for only four hours a day and I was making three dollars an hour. I worked there for a full year, until a friend told that I should apply for a job at the restaurant where she worked. When you are first here, it is difficult to know where to look for work. Anyway, they finally hired me as a kitchen helper.

I went back to the motel, and told the owner that I was going to stop working there because I now had a full-time job. He said, "Where?" I said "In a restaurant." He said, "Oh ya, you'll probably be washing dishes." You know, that is the attitude they have - that our people only wash dishes. I still remember that. I will always remember that.

I was taking classes all the time then; that's how my English improved.

I worked in the kitchen so I didn't have to deal with the customers. It was mostly our people in the kitchen. The waitress and carhops were all white. I always felt like something was going on. For example, when the waitresses have to ask other white people for something, they smile and speak nicely, but when they have to talk to us, they don't smile at all, and are very rude. I've noticed that.

I'm now working as a nurse's aide. If I had a choice, I would like a more creative job: even working in the office. I wouldn't do this work if I had a choice. The work is not any better, but it is better paying; we have a union and benefits.

I wish I could continue to learn English, so that I could say what I feel like inside. Right now, I can't. Many times, I find myself stuck for words. I want to be good in English so that I can get a good job. Now I know what other women are doing and I know I can do the work, but I think I will have some problems communicating with others. I think the other people think you are dumb if you cannot communicate with them.

Pamela Godfree

Karen Pheasant

I am from Manitoulin Island. My mother is Odawa and my father is Ojibway. They left the reserve like a lot of people did about thirty years ago. During that period there was a heavy migration of Native people into the cities. The church came to the reserves about one hundred and fifty years ago; before that we had our own way of life. Often we were referred to as being pagans or savages, but we had our tradition.

My parents and a lot of people in their age group were automatically taken away from their homes at the age of six and taken into residential schools for ten years. Our people lost a lot of their traditional living styles like hunting and the support system of their family.

During that time alcohol was introduced to the native people by the Europeans. They used it as a way to get to us. "Once those Native people are drunk, then we can take their furs." For the longest time there was law that said Indians were not allowed in bars; it has only been in the last thirty or forty years that Indians have been allowed in bars, even in Toronto. It was against the Indian Act to sell liquor to native people. We never learned to use booze.

My mom and dad got married on the reserve. The importance of education was instilled upon families like my mom's and dad's. My mom went on to get a nursing education. She (and all native children), had a hard time in the residential schools in terms of their Native identity. She was punished for speaking her language and made to feel really inadequate and low about being Native. At that time, my mother made a promise to herself that if she ever had children, they would know the English language, have an education and also have the opportunities which are important to the dominant society. I was born here in the city (I have a brother and sister also). My mother put aside the traditional culture that her mother had taught her when she worked in the city. My mom and dad have always worked. They bought a house, a car and they stressed the importance of education upon the three of us kids.

I started hanging with the Friendship Centre when I was fifteen, getting involved in the youth group. It was when I started being with my own people and developing a positive self-identity that I realized that it wasn't important to have formal education. What was more important to me was being a strong Native person. I completed high school and got married, had a boy and girl. My brother and sister also finished high school but that's as far as we got. As soon as I got my grade twelve, I came here to the centre. I started volunteering in the centre, and then I worked as a summer student. One thing led to another - eventually I got the job as Director of Programmes. I feel I've accomplished many things here, and I've postponed thoughts of going to university at present.

There are Friendship Centres in every town and city across Canada, from Halifax to Victoria Island, and way up to Yellowknife. We have a National Association of Friendship Centres. They started twenty-five years ago, and during that time they were a place to assist native people who migrated into the city. They helped them to go about getting jobs, housing, education, etc. But now Native people have been in the cities for so long that their needs have changed. They've lost their cultural ties. So the new role of Friendship Centres is "cultural retention." Also the role is to develop leadership abilities within our people, to make them capable of doing things for themselves. Not only must you develop your people, but you must develop the organization in which you work, the structure of it.

During the past year that I've been acting as Executive Director, I have learned a lot of management and technical skills, which had it not been for the encouragement and support of people at the centre, I would not have learned. During the summer of '79, when I started working here, there was a study done on Native families in the city. I was one of the interviewers - I walked a lot of streets and knocked on lots of doors and listened to a lot of people. Those are my qualifications for working here. When I first started there was no children's program here. We now have a nursery school, an after-school program, a youth program, a supper program, and a driver and family worker. There's no other native children's program in Canada. There have been attempts, but no full program. Here we have babies to teenagers. We worked hard for it ... a real long fight. There's also a women's political group and a women's quilting group. I've been a part of it all. It's running with a few wrinkles but it's there and the funding is pretty well secure.

I'm a single parent. We've been on our own for three years, the children and I. Last summer I took two weeks off and we went to Regina to the World Assembly of First Nations, to Montana and B.C., Saskatchewan - all over. Just us three. That started me thinking about leaving the city. "Hey, there's a whole world out there." I have a lot of living to do, especially in the learning of our tradition and culture. I want to learn my language. I want to spend time with the old people. When I was a little kid, I was desperate to learn Ojibway, but my parents didn't speak it to us. Now I can understand Ojibway quite a bit but I only speak it with the old people 'cause they don't laugh at me. They know I'm trying; people your own age tend to laugh at you.

The elders say that cities aren't a place to live. They don't say it directly, but they talk about what goes on in the cities, that it can't be good. When I visit with the elders, they talk about having respect for our mother - Mother Earth. She's the one who feeds and clothes us; the rivers and streams in her body are the stream of life. What they are doing to her is like raping her, treating her with no respect. And if you really want to be close with her and live in balance with yourself, it's good to get out of the cities, go back to where you can go for a walk, hear her talking and listen to the water. My kids know nothing but the city life even though they spend their summers and holidays on the reserve. Even they say it's noisy in the city. Last Sunday we went up to Georgian Bay...it was so free...running and shouting and Mathew was just smiling, ear to ear. They're five and seven years.

Sophie started grade one last September and her first couple of weeks were so...oh, the ignorance of children in the schools and around ethnic kids. Already she's experiencing racism. She told me they tease her because she is an Indian. She has this T-shirt with an Indian dancer on it. She is so proud of that. I took her to pow wows this summer so that she could feel good about herself. So, she went to school, so proud, wearing the T-shirt and the children just cut her up, shot her down. They started dancing how they felt Indians did. She was so hurt that she never wanted to go back to school. I tried to tell her that she had to go back; it was very hard. But I know that we can't just pack up and go somewhere else and think that she wouldn't be teased again. But I want to leave the city. I'm not necessarily going back to the reserve, but I want to give my kids a taste of different lifestyles. It will be up to them to choose. It's only in the last few years that I'm learning about the spiritual ways. They'll know the right thing when they're older and they won't go through that period of identity crisis as I did. I've shown them both sides.

My husband and I are not together. He was into drinking, so I had to deal with other things. I had chosen a career in working with our people. During the marriage, I realized that I couldn't cook and clean and do the laundry - there had to be expectations from both of us. He had to wash dishes and do his part. He didn't like doing that. His idea was maybe what he'd seen on T.V., or what he read. "I bring home a paycheck and you do the other things." Things didn't work out. That's the difference from my grandmother and mother - they stayed in their relationships no matter what.

My parents feel they've accomplished what they wanted here. They're selling their house, finally, after thirty years; they have a cabin and land up north on a reserve. So they're going back to their roots. I've had the opportunity of being raised here and because I've been on the reserve, back and forth so many times, I'm not naive to reserve life. I'm aware of reserve living, rural living. I'm going back, I'm leaving here this Spring.

I've been involved in the centre for ten years and I think it's time to move on. My mom couldn't understand it, she said, "why are you gonna leave, what about your kids' education?" But education in one person's eyes is not the same as in another's. I think it's good for me to move on. Sometimes you're in an organization or situation for so long that you can't be objective about it - you're right in the whirlwind. You begin to lose your sight, and you become cynical. You don't realise that you've built a dependency on your organisation, and that maybe it's time for the leadership that we've been developing in the youths to take over. That's why I decided to leave. I've taken so much and I can only give so much. I think someone can come in with new skills and expertise and add a breath of fresh air. I can go to another centre. I have a strong commitment to the Friendship Centre movement. People living in the city have to have a community behind them - the centre is the community. I'd like to go around and share what skills I have and continue in other centres in other towns.

silenced

Makeda Silvera

Talks with working class West Indian
women about their lives and struggles
as Domestic Workers in Canada.

The following is an excerpt from SILENCED by Makeda Silvera, a book of oral interviews with West Indian Domestic Workers on the Temporary Employment Visa. In the interviews, the women talk about their own lives, their visions and struggles, and what it means to be temporary workers in Canada.

"Ever Since I Can Remember Life Was Rough"

I started working on the work permit in 1978, but that was not the first time I came to Canada. The first time was in 1973, but I was on the go.[1] The idea to come to Canada was really started with my friend. We were really good friends in Jamaica, we went everywhere together. We even had our babies around the same time.

Well she and I use to always talk about coming to Canada as tourists and then staying on to work as domestics.

Things were not really working out for us in Jamaica. Most of the time we couldn't find work and we had our children to feed and send to school. Ever since I can remember life was rough for me, even as a girl growing up. We grew up in the country, a place called St. Thomas, but I left St. Thomas when I was about 14 years old. I went to Kingston[2] to stay with an aunt and to find work. I didn't even finish high school. My family couldn't afford to school all of us, especially us girls. But I was glad not to have to go to school because I use to have to walk barefoot for about six miles back and forth everyday to go to school. It was really embarrassing, especially when we had to pass boys on the way to school.

When first I went to Kingston I stayed with my aunt and I worked with a lady looking after her children and cleaning and cooking for her. When I was about 16 years old I met my boyfriend who I have my children for and eventually I moved out of my aunt to live with him. I had some really bad times in Kingston, trying to find work, making enough money for my family to live on. Sometimes it got really rough. I remember I use to just sit and cry some days when I couldn't find the money to buy food for my children. My boyfriend wasn't working most of the times and so everybody depended on me. That's when I decided to come to Canada.

My girlfriend had another friend who was a domestic worker in Montreal and she eventually left Jamaica to go there. A few months after she left I bought my ticket as a tourist and came to Toronto. This was in 1973. When I came to Immigration they questioned me for over an hour and finally they let me through and I went and found a hotel to sleep that night. The next morning I got somebody to direct me. I went to Bay Street and I took the Gray Coach to Montreal. I was all alone by myself and frightened. But when I got to Montreal I asked questions and then took a taxi to where my friend was living. I didn't stay with her for long, I felt a little bit shy staying with her because I didn't know her friend that she was staying with, and then she wasn't adjusted to the place so we didn't get on the same way we did in Jamaica. I wasn't happy in Montreal and it was hard to find work because I don't speak French. Soon after that I met another Jamaican girl in Montreal and became friends with her. She told me her mother lived around Dufferin and King Street in Toronto and she asked me if I wanted to come to Toronto with her. I said yes.

"The Work Was Hard, The Hours Was Long And The Pay Lousy"

We came back together and I stayed with her and her mother for awhile. They were very nice to me. Whenever my friend got jobs for herself, she would take one and give me one. Once she got me a job with some people, but I didn't stay there long because the people didn't want to pay me and sometimes I didn't even get enough to eat. So I just stayed there a little while and then I left.

Eventually I meet some new friends through this same girlfriend of mine. I remember one of my new friends were doing a job around Richmond Hill[3] for about $25 a week and she decided to give it to mc bccausc shc found a better job. You know something, when I started working with this lady she never paid me the full $25. She knew I wasn't landed, that I wasn't on a work permit, that I was here illegally and that I couldn't complain to anybody so she just kept on giving me the $20 a week. I work hard for that money - cleaning the floors, washing dishes, washing clothes and looking after two young children. I was living-in so I was like on call 24 hours a day.

By 1974 I was disgusted and fed up of that kind of life, hiding from Immigration, not being able to speak up for my rights. Plus I was feeling very lonely. I was missing my boyfriend and my three children. (Right now my children are 13, 12 and 10 years old. I send money for them regularly, but oh god, I miss them. When I left in 1973 my youngest child was nine months old. I know that whenever we meet again he won't even know me. It hurts.)

But I knew that I couldn't go home because maybe I wouldn't be so lucky the next time coming through Immigration. So again I left that job and tried to find something in a little better condition. I put an ad in the paper to find another job, but I got so much crank calls that I had to take the ads out.

A friend of mine who was working at Mayfair Mansion (a Toronto apartment block) told me they were looking for people and to apply. I got the job and stayed there for about a year and some weeks. I eventually left there too. It was the same story - the work was hard and the hours was long and the pay lousy. When I left Mayfair I got another little cleaning job to do - go around to different offices at night and clean. The company use to take us out on cleaning jobs. But sometimes for two week, we only got $40 a week. Sometimes you might go there everyday for the two week and you might go on a cleaning job for only three nights. So you end up wasting a lot of time sitting around waiting to see if they will call you. The thing is you had to go there every night and sit and wait to see if any cleaning jobs come in. But I think they had their favourites who they give the jobs to. Boy with that job, I thought I was going out of my mind because there was just not enough money.

"I Had A Aim In View"

Eventually I met a friend who worked at Toronto Western Hospital who told me about a patient who was going home and needed somebody to look after her. She told me she would make the arrangements for me. She did and I went on the interview.

I remember it was a Sunday and she was kind of nervous with me, I guess because she was alone and an old woman. So I started working. I eventually start to work with her from March 1976, then I went back home in 1978 and she applied to Manpower and Immigration and took me back legally on a work permit. I stayed and worked with her until she died in August 1981. She was 83 years old when she died. I really missed her. Of course, we did have our little misunderstanding through the years that I work with her, but I tell you of all the people I worked with, she was the best.

I use to get $118 a week. It could have been more, but I was satisfied. I figured it was only her alone that I had to look after and you know it wasn't that much work. I didn't wash for her. Her clothes went to the laundry, except for those soiled up which I washed. I cooked for her and I did the dusting around the house. There was another lady who came in once week to do the heavy house cleaning. So the hardest thing really was changing her clothes when she eventually became incontinent. But I was very grateful for the job and the $118 a week. Like I said, she was a nice lady and in a lot of ways I was more like a companion to her. She had a lot of nieces and nephews but they did not visit her a lot. I remember her niece use to say to me that she doesn't know how I stand her aunt. None of her nieces ever stayed longer than 15 minutes with her. Sometimes she acted kind of weird and I guess they were frightened. She used to make a lot of noises like "whoo, whoo, whooooo" day and night. Sometimes, I had to close my door and my room was right in front of hers, so closing the door didn't block out the noise. But I had a aim in view, so I didn't get fed up and leave the job. Not that I was using the job or her as a convenience. But I knew what I wanted and she needed. Both of us needed each other. She had no children and her husband had died twenty-one years ago. So it was just the two of us in the house and then later my little baby.

Her friends and relatives hardly came to see her. They said that she was too miserable and that every time they came there all they could hear about was how sick she was so they kept away from her. During those times I was the closest one to her. I was a companion to her. I listened to her when she talked. Read to her. Brush her hair for her. Made sure she took her medication. Fed her, you know - things like that. But it comes a time about six months before she died when she became incontinent. She did everything in bed. So I had to do everything for her then. Like tidy her off, clean up the bed, just be around her whenever she wanted me. The housekeeper still came in once a week, but otherwise I had to do everything for her. You know, it was probably all those things, like lifting her onto the bed when she fell was why I had to eventually go in the hospital with a hernia - I had to lift her so many times.

One of the reasons why I really liked Mrs. Tucker[4] and put up with all of that during the last months was because she really gave me the chance to get on the work permit. Plus when I came back on the work permit in 1978 I was three months pregnant which I didn't tell her because I was afraid that if she found out she wouldn't hire me. But when she found out, she didn't run me from the job.

Boy, I really went through a lot in this country. I remember the night when I set in to have the baby. I remember when the pain took me one night I was in her room. I had to kneel down on the floor at her bedside because the pain was really so awful. I remember I told her I had to go to the hospital. She phoned her minister and told him that I fainted. When I got to the hospital she phoned and they told her that I had a little baby boy. Looking back on it now, I can't really see how she didn't see that I was pregnant. She could see and she could hear pretty good, but she was conveniently deaf and blind when she wanted to. After I had the baby, I came out of the hospital and I continued to look after Mrs. Tucker and I brought home the baby with me. Mrs. Tucker was still a little shocked when I came home with the baby, but still she overcome that. She get to - not admit - she get to accept it. As a matter of fact she even named the baby.

"I Needed A Job Or They Would Deport Me"

After she passed away I had to find another job. The next job I got was the worst job I have ever had since I come to Canada. It was a job working at a home for ex-mental patients. I didn't know anything about my employer or the job when I took the job. Time was running out for me, my visa was going to be expired and so I needed to be in a job or they would deport me. This was September '81 and my visa would run out by October '81. Mrs Tucker was dead and I needed to have a job. That job was really awful. Working with Mrs. Tucker during the last months of her life was one hundred per cent better than this last job. So that should show you how bad it was. This woman (the new employer) didn't respect people who worked with her. She treated everybody like a dog.

I remember that I took sick the sixth month I was working with this new woman. I was sick with a hernia problem and I had to go into the hospital. They told me that I had to get surgery in my belly button. This was the pain that had been hurting me on and off for the past two years since I was with Mrs. Tucker. The night I took in with the hernia I was on the job and I was scared. Before it would always hurt and stop. Sometimes it use to hurt and then it would swell big - big like a rock - but then it would always go right back in after I put hot water on it. This time the pain started from the Tuesday and by Thursday, I couldn't even take the street car home. I had to get a friend to take me to the doctor. He told me it was bad and that I should go to the emergency section of the Doctor's Hospital. Boy, I'm telling you, I would never like to got through all that pain again - it was kind of horrible. Because I was to have surgery, I had to stay in the hospital for a couple of days. Well, on the third day that I was in the hospital, I heard that my employer got another new girl to fill my vacancy. It was two of us girls who always work in the home. So on the third day she got another new girl. She didn't even say anything to me and she knew where I was. I stayed six days in the hospital. When I came out I spoke to Mrs

Smith[5], my employer, on the telephone and she didn't ask me to come back. She didn't say anything to me about the job. She didn't say anything. I was so hurt. It was as if she use me and I am of no more service so forget about me and find somebody else to do the job.

Let me tell you about my job with her for the six months. There were two of us who usually work there at the house. We were in charge of the 30 patients. And one of us usually had to sleep over with them. Mrs. Smith hardly ever came down to the house unless to supervise or complain about something we did wrong. The house was a very big house - it had three floor. Some of the rooms had four to five beds each. The patients all ate downstairs in the basement. There were about five table down there and then there were bathrooms on each floor. We had to do almost everything in that house - cook, clean, wash, scrub the floors, give the patients their medication. You name it - we had to do it. It was dreadful like hell there. It was very tense in the house because a lot of the patients are ex-mental patients from 999[6] and sometimes, if they didn't take their medication, they could get violent and attack us. We had to be calling the police almost every day. They (the police) use to tell us that what we are doing is a man's job. They use to say that a man should be there with us. But because Mrs Smith didn't want to pay out the extra money, she only had us two girls there to do all the work every day.

I was going crazy in that job. I use to get $85 a week. I was going off my head because that job just couldn't support me and the baby. I was boarding him out for $50 a week, plus I still had to send money for my three children back home. So because of that I had to take up another job too. I was at the boarding house from eight in the morning to around seven at night. Then I would go to another cleaning job from nine at night to six in the morning. I use to get no sleep. I tell you I was going crazy. But I had to keep it up because I had to be paying out so much bills. I was hardly saving any money because I had to send home money too. Plus the $50 for the baby, plus pay my rent. Sometimes I had to even sleep over at the boarding house. That was when the other girl who live in had her days off and Mrs. Smith wanted somebody there for the weekend.

I remember there was a high turn-over of girls there at the home. Girls use to quit every two weeks or so, but as soon as they quit Mrs. Smith would find somebody else to take their place. Nobody stayed at that place very long. They quit as fast as they come. And there's always other girls to fill their vacancy. This is why when I got sick she didn't care whether I came back or not, because she knew she could get another girl with no problem.

Even now she have money for me. I remember I went into the hospital the Thursday evening and I was suppose to get paid the Friday, and until now - it's three months now - I haven't got my money from her yet. I phoned and left a message with the new girl that is working there. I said to her, "Please tell Mrs. Smith to leave my money. I will come and picks it up." She hasn't left my money yet. I really need the money because I need to look after my little boy here and my three children in Jamaica.

The other day I was telling a friend of mine about Mrs. Smith and the meagre salary she was paying me. My friend was asking how she manage to get away with it from Manpower. But the thing is, Manpower don't know because she told Manpower she was paying me $100 a week. It's on the paper, it's written down in the contract.

Stephanie Martin

When I started working with her she told me she was paying me $85 a week. She is a crook and she thinks she is smart. She thinks I don't know. But I knew what was going on. She is so ungrateful. She knew she was paying me less than I'm suppose to get. And because I get sick and have to go to the hospital, she get someone else. She didn't even care if I eat or have a place to live.

I'm telling you, in a way I'm glad she didn't ask me to come back. I don't want anything else to do with that woman. All I want from her now is my money. I just want to forget about her.

"We're Doing The Dirty Work"

Some employers are good and some don't care much about you. All they want to do is to work you like a slave and as soon as anything happen to you whether on the job or not, that's it. That's it. They want no part of you. But thank god, all of them are not the same because Mrs. Tucker wasn't like that. I'm not expecting all of them to be the same, but show a little gratitude. Show your appreciation. We're doing the dirty work. They are paying the money. But they think probably we are nobody. They must treat us equal, like we are human beings too, not like some animal.

My experience with Mrs. Smith make me feel very bitter.

Well, I'm going to put an ad in the papers Friday, Saturday and Sunday. I don't know if it will help, but I would really like to get another job soon. Maybe I'll even have to take one live-in. I don't like those jobs, though. It's not nice living-in at people's houses. They don't treat us with any kindness or understanding. Sometimes, what they give us to eat is not even sufficient, not even nourishing. The other thing is that we doesn't have privacy in the houses. They come and knock us up every time they can't find something no matter what time it is. We have to be right there until they fall asleep. These things are not fair.

It would be nice if we were allowed to rent a room of our own. Some of us would feel better about domestic work if we could come out of their home and go home to our home. It's really not nice the way they treat us. We don't have much choice because you come from another country and you don't know anybody here. After you are here a little time and you have friends, Manpower and Immigration should allow you to rent a place of you own. Because after you are here a little time and you make friends, then you want your own social life. You want to work in the days and go home in the nights like anybody else.

Some of us have been here four, five, six years and still living in people's basements or sharing rooms with small children. I know people who are stuck in people's houses for eight years. My god. I really feel sorry for them. Most of them can't take their friends there. You have no social life, and if you even go out for Sunday, by Sunday night you have to be back in. It's not really lovely.

"Just Half Way Through My Journey, I Still Have Another Half To Go"

I'm just praying I get a job soon and that it is a job that I can live-out. If not, I'll have to take a live-in. Right now, I pay $130 a month for this room and I share the kitchen and bathroom with someone else. I feel a little more comfortable having my own room and having my privacy. If I had my landed, though, I would feel much better because then I could go any place. I could look for any kind of job I wanted. Even now, we are not allowed to take factory jobs, only domestic work.[7]

I'm just crossing my fingers that I will get my landed soon. I apply for landed status but I don't hear anything. I'm just counting the months. I miss my children, but I can't go down to look for them until I get my landed. I wish I could have them here with me - loneliness - it's almost like a crime. It makes you feel so, so helpless, so vulnerable, so ashamed. It's almost like a crime. The only socializing I really do is go to church. Right now, I'm involved in the Domestic Workers Group and so we meet once a month. That really comes in handy because it eases the loneliness.

Sometimes when I talk to some of my girlfriends, I tell them to try to join a church group or the Domestic Workers Group, but a lot of them don't take this advice. We just prefer to stay in our own little small world by ourselves, we don't want to get involved. But I keep telling them that if they don't go out, they won't know what's going on. Like the last time I went down to Immigration, they kept asking me if I belonged to any church or group. I think they ask you those things because they want to know if anything happens to you how you are going to manage. But a lot of girls are kind of confused. Are we suppose to join groups or are we not suppose to? Some girls believe if you join a group you might make it bad for yourself. They feel that maybe the Immigration won't like this.

I just hope that I get this landed. They say it would take about a year. I'm praying I get it soon. It's been a real struggle, believe me. But I made up my mind to stick it out because I've gone a long way and I can't turn back now. It's hard in Jamaica for a lot of people. That why we come here and even when we come here there is still the hardship. Sometimes you don't even know who to trust. I have this friend who hired a lawyer and the lawyer charged her $800 just to go down to Immigration with her. She is on a work permit too and she applied once for landed and they turned her down. I don't know why she went to the lawyer because she could apply on her own. Boy, $800 just for him to take her down one time to say three little words.

Right now, I'm trying to get into George Brown College to take a course in Health Care Aide. In order to get your landed they want you to show them a certificate. To apply to do the course they want to dip deep down in your background. And you don't even know what they want to know.

Stephanie Martin

Each part of the course cost $70 and there are about six different parts. The course really cost $35, but because they're charging us foreign student rate I have to pay $70 for each part.

Like I said, life here in Canada has been a real struggle. But I just make up my mind to stick it out because I've been a long way since I came here first in 1973. When I finish this course at George Brown and get the certificate that means I can go and work in any institution - like a hospital or look after the elderly. I wouldn't want to stay in domestic work when I finish school and get my landed. No way. I would get out of it so fast that nobody would believe it.

When I get my landed I would like to send for the kids and my boyfriend. He does construction work back home and I know he would get a job if he came up. I'd be so happy because I wouldn't have to hustle so much, because I've been doing a lot of it in this country. All by myself. Sometimes I feel tired. I need some help. I says to myself, if he were here, I wouldn't even have to think of looking for a job right away. I could stay home with the baby for awhile. Now that I board him out, I hardly seen him - only on weekends. I just hope everything work out fine and I get the landed and my family get to come up. I want to start living like a normal person with my family.

"Just To Feel More Free"

It's been such a hard struggle with the Immigration. I only hope they don't reject my application. It would be so nice to feel free. Not that I am not free, because I don't feel like a criminal, but just to feel more free. Free to go anywhere I want to go. Free to look for any kind of job I want. God I just hope something might come through quick. I've been struggling for so long that sometimes I wonder if it will ever end or if this is to be my life. It seems so long.

It's not easy I tell you, leaving your country and coming to this country to work. It's not easy. But if you leave your country with a dream, you just have to make up you mind that you want that dream to come through some day. You know, a lot of us come here as illegal immigrants and we are not free. We are like prisoners and we hide and hope that one day we will be like normal human beings.

I was like that once too, and now, thank god, I'm not one hundred per cent free, but I know now that I don't have to hide. I can open the door if the doorbell rings. When I walk on the street I don't have to keep looking back unless I expect someone. I don't have to look for a police car or look at anybody funny. When I was here the first time without the permit, I felt terrified and a lot of times I felt like dying. You know, like when you hear the doorbell and don't know whether to answer it or not. I'm telling you, it can really wrankle your nerves.

But, like I always say, things and time have a way of working out itself and sometimes you just have to wait on time. Just be patient. I have been waiting for the past nine years in this country and I'm just half way there. Just half way through my journey, I still have another half to go.

I don't know when it will end, but I am still going to hang in there because I still have hopes and I feel I've been through the worst.

Footnotes

1. Without landed status or a work permit.
2. Capital of Jamaica.
3. Upper middle class area of Toronto.
4. Not her real name.
5. Not her real name to protect the victim.
6. The Queen Street Mental Health Centre in Toronto.
7. While on a work permit.

A Poem by **Sylvia Hamilton**

Someone's Old Favorite

I don't remember

the first time I was called it

how old I was, what day it was,

who said it and why.

Only that it happened enough other times

the first doesn't matter any more.

And now, on my twenty-sixth birthday,

out of the anonymity of the night

came the familiar sound from a passing car

(N-I-G-G-E-RRRRRRRR)

which once again accompanied me home.

Two Feminist Fables by **Suniti Namjoshi**

From the Panchatantra

In the holy city of Benares there lived a brahmin, who, as he walked by the riverbank, watching the crows floating downstream, feeding on the remains of half-burnt corpses, consoled himself thus: 'It is true that I am poor, but I am a brahmin, it is true that I have no sons, but I, myself, am indisputably a male. I shall return to the temple and pray to Lord Vishnu to grant me a son.' He went off to the temple and Lord Vishnu listened and Lord Vishnu complied, but whether through absent-mindedness or whether for some other more abstruse reason, he gave him a daughter. The brahmin was disappointed. When the child was old enough, he called her to him and delivered himself thus: 'I am a brahmin. You are my daughter. I had hoped for a son. No matter. I will teach you what I know, and when you are able, we will both meditate and seek guidance.' Though only a woman, she was a brahmin, so she learned very fast, and then, they both sat down and meditated hard. In a very short time Lord Vishnu appeared. 'What do you want?' he said. The brahmin couldn't stop himself. He blurted out quickly, 'I want a son.' 'Very well.' said the god, 'Next time around.' In his next incarnation the brahmin was a woman and bore eight sons. 'And what do you want he said to the girl. 'I want human status.' 'Ah, that is much harder,' and the god hedged and appointed a commission.

The *Panchatantra* is a Sanskrit book of fables. Unlike Aesop's it contains both brahmins and beasts.

The Fox and the Stork

One day a fox invited a stork for a visit. As soon as Stork arrived, Fox started saying that she, herself, was a very progressive fox and intended fully to respect Stork and Stork's individuality. 'Thank you,' said Stork. 'Now,' said Fox, 'I do not wish to make any assumptions, and so I must ask you: do Storks, in fact, eat?' 'Yes,' said Stork. 'How extraordinary,' said Fox, 'and do they eat food, or do they eat some amazing and unlikely dish?' 'We eat some amazing and unlikely dish,' said Stork. 'How delightful,' said Fox, 'how absolutely charming.' 'And tell me,' she added, 'have Storks ever been known to drink?' 'We drink on the fifth and seventh of each month, except in leap year, when we drink on the third and fourteenth respectively.' 'How curious,' said Fox, 'how very interesting. And can Storks speak? I mean, I see that you are speaking, but are Storks fluent in ordinary speech?' 'No,' said Stork shaking her head sadly, 'we ration words, and I've used up mine for at least three centuries. I must be leaving,' and left abruptly.

In her work on Storks, Fox has computed that the average stork utters seventeen words, exactly seventeen, in every century.

LESBIANS OF COLOUR: LOVING AND STRUGGLING

"A conversation between three lesbians of colour"

Joanne: Why don't we want to use our real names?

Pramila: It's all so complicated.

Anu: I haven't come out to anybody except my closest friends. And I don't plan on coming out at this time to my community (East Indian) or to my family. I think that if my parents found out, or my siblings, they would reject me and I would be isolated. Until recently, my family was the only place of refuge, of comfort, of love that I have had in Canada. We have a shared experience and understanding. When we first came to Canada form Guyana we felt very much alone in Canadian society. You see, we came to Toronto before the racist immigration policies were changed and more East Indians were allowed into the country. Wherever we went, we were the first of our people. My brothers and sisters were the first East Indians in the schools where we lived, we were the first East Indians to move into the neighbourhood. At that time, there were no community organizations so we were very much on our own.

There are moments when I think that my family would support me if I told them I was a lesbian. They have a very strong belief in family, they also know that we live in a place where we are isolated (in so many ways) and that "we only have each other," as they keep reminding me. So maybe they would support me...?

Joanne: If you do tell them, let me know. I would be interested in knowing what happens.

Anu: I know this is a rhetorical question, but why don't you want to use your real name?

Joanne: I work for the government in one of the social service departments and most of my co-workers are white and fairly open about sexuality. So a few of them know that I am a lesbian. But you see, most of my work is done in the Black community and I know that if they found out it would be hard for me: I could easily be ostracised within the Black community, I don't believe clients would respect my work. It's really unbelievable how rampant homophobia is within the Black community . Sometimes I feel I live in two worlds. With my friends who I'm 'out' to I feel comfortable. I havve no fears. With certain sections of the Black community and my family, I feel really uptight - wondering when they will find out.

Another reason why I'm so hesitant to come out is because of my twelve year old daughter. I want to talk about my sexual preference with her before I come out to the world. You see, lesbianism is something relatively new for me, like I didn't know when I was fourteen or sixteen years old that I would be woman-identified or that I would want to spend my life with women. So for me it's like something new and I really want to spend the time to work out my feelings and be comfortable with the choice I've made before I'm exposed to the coldness of the larger society. It's really important for me to work it out, to give myself a chance with the person that I'm involved with and to work with my daughter. It's really such a crucial age for her too, she has reached adolescence and she has her own little world to deal with. At this point, I don't want to confuse her and I don't want her to be hostile towards me.

Joanne: What about your community Pramila, do they know?

Pramila: There are some women that know. I used to be part of a women's group in my community and some of the women in that group knew. All my sisters and cousins know, but my parents and older relatives don't know.

Joanne: Do you think you would be isolated if they found out? I mean by both your family and the Indian community?

Pramila: Most definitely, and I do feel isolated. One, because I'm a lesbian and two because the woman I'm involved with is white. In our community there's a whole way of relating with friends and extended families, you know, friends become like family. And I feel a lot of reluctance from the woman I'm involved with to be any part of that. On the one hand she feels that she wants to be - but I feel that because she is so unclear about how much of my life she wants to be a part of, that it makes things difficult. If I have a social event to go to, she will be reluctant to come because she might be the only white person there, and it becomes a real hassle to be always pulling her around with me, especially when she herself is so up and down about it, and so totally insecure about relating to a whole other culture. But, then, they never think what it's like for us. We have to spend all our lives in a white culture. So, you know, sometimes I really feel isolated... and because of my lifestyle I could never live in an Indian ghetto neighbourhood. Because I feel that I could not live as a lesbian there. There would be too many restrictions and who needs more hassles?

I really value the sort of work I do, which is working with my community. I'm really committed to my community, and I feel that if they found out it could create problems. So, in a sense, I really have no place where I sort of touch base in any way.

Joanne: It's really quite sad, you know. I mean, we are isolated from our communities because of our sexual preference. And the support we need we often don't get from the feminist/lesbian community. We experience so much racism from within the women's community.

Anu: Yes, and another thing we have to deal with is our invisibility, which is part of their racism; they usually don't see us as lesbians. I remember I was applying for a job a few summers ago within a feminist organization and I was competing for the job with a white lesbian. I was hired over her. Later on, I heard that I was hired because they "already had enough lesbians," and so they didn't need any more, but what they did need was a woman of colour because they had no contacts in these communities. They hadn't even asked me in the interview if I was involved in my community or in any other women of colour communities. They were buying themselves a ready-made full-fledged woman of colour to make contact with the women of colour communities.

Joanne: That's very interesting and so typical.

Anu: When they hired me their underlying assumption was that a woman of colour could not be a lesbian. In their minds, these two things were mutually exclusive. They just assumed that I was straight and they never checked it out with me. During the interview one woman asked me if I would have problems working with lesbian women. Even after I started working with the women as a group they overlooked every instance that could point to the fact that I was woman-identified. I live with a woman and they know that, but they haven't made the connection yet.

I've decided not to identify myself as a lesbian with white women anymore. When I do tell white lesbians/straights that I am a lesbian, I am met with curious disbelief. Or they begin to regard me in a sexually racist way - I'm exotic, a novelty, a toy....

I think one of the other reasons that the women that I work with don't see me as a lesbian is because they can't see through the myth and that myth is: women of colour are male-identified. I remember that summer a lot of the women saw me around town with a very good male friend of mine (we're from the same community), and I can see how that possibly has fed into their myths about male-identification.

Pramila: And the way we dress also feeds into their idea of us as heterosexual women. There are a lot of unspoken and unwritten laws in the lesbian society of how to dress and how to look. I think that most of us are not able to fit in a very clean-cut way into these categories: of having short hair, being white, you know, plaid shirts and boots. And if you are not conforming, if you don't fit into those laws and those definitions of how to dress and behave, then you are not so easily identified as lesbian.

Anu: I'm never going to cut my hair again....

Pramila: When we look at who we are and what our culture is, and how we dress, most of us are not going to fit in. And I think that puts us even farther apart. But I'm sure that if you, Anu, were to cut your hair and dress up like the norms dictate, you know, very butch and all that, you would be considered lesbian. I think the problem is that, for example, women in saris and salwar kameez would never be seen as lesbians. One night I was taking a feminist from India to a number of gay bars in Toronto, and she was wearing Indian clothes and I was wearing Indian clothes and we were with a Japanese women...

Anu: ...and they figured you walked into the wrong bar, right?

(*laughter*)

*   *   *   *   *

Joanne: Anu, earlier on you had started talking about something that is very interesting and very popular in the women's community: the concept of women of colour being male-identified.

Anu: I feel that so strongly, that that is what they think...

Pramila: What do you mean male-identified? You don't mean heterosexual?

Anu: That we are always thinking about men.

Joanne: Always think about *our* men, not white men. Always protecting *our* men.

Pramila: Against white women?

Joanne: Against white people.

Anu: I've been in lots of situations where women have said to me, "Why are you always talking about yourself as a group?" I guess it's that notion that Shulamith Firestone, and a number of other feminist writers and theoreticians have put out, that sexism is more of a fundamental problem than racism, and I guess that goes very deep into white women's consciousness, they're raised to believe that.

Joanne: Yeah, and the books really put that out, and also the Women's Studies courses...so it's really easy for them to say, "ignore the race business." Their history is just so completely different from ours that they can afford to separate themselves from their men, and I support them, but *we* can't afford to....

Pramila: I think that one of the reasons that they can separate themselves from their men is that most of them live in very exclusive small lesbian sub-cultures. Most of us also live in the lesbian sub-culture, but we also live in a whole other mainstream society and we are people of colour and so it makes absolutely no sense to only function on the premise that you work only with women or that you only address women's problems.

Joanne: No, how can we separate when we have a history of oppression and exploitation as a people? When the Ku Klux Klan attacks, or any other rightwingers for that matter, they don't just attack women of colour, they attack our men and children.

Pramila: There's an incident that happened to me that I'd like to share with you. It's to do with this male friend of mine. We spend quite a bit of time together. Well! This white woman I know, said to me one day that, "Oh, so I see that you are taking care of _____." She said it like a put down. That here I was, a woman, getting sucked into looking after this man. And isn't that what women end up doing all the time, anyway. Meaning that I was playing the traditional role of women.
    What she fails to see is that we both care for each other and that maybe I *want* to put out to him. And that maybe he also puts out to me. Also, if I had a similar relationship with a woman it would never be questioned. I think this example typifies the problem of men between women of colour and white women.

*   *   *   *   *

Joanne: How hard is it to come out to each other as lesbians, and also to come out to our own community?

Anu: I don't think people, in general, understand what it's like to be a lesbian of colour in this society and how difficult it is to come out. I am not negating the fact that it is difficult for all lesbians to come out, but for women of colour, I think that there are some special problems that we face.

What I would like to stress the most is that women of colour, lesbians of colour, have essentially, a smaller community of people that we can expect support from, so to us it is a big risk to jeopardize that community. For if all that we have left is the lesbian community, then we are in big trouble. No matter how much they would like to believe otherwise, the lesbian community is still a representation of the larger society, infected with the same sorts of diseases: racism, classism.

I would like to relate an experience of mine to you. I went to conference not too long ago on Third World Women and Feminism. A white women approached me and started to tell me about her relationship with an East Indian woman who now lives in Toronto.

She told me about how she felt the woman was cowardly for not "coming out," for not choosing to live a "lesbian lifestyle." I became really angry with this woman and took her to task for her racism, her non-understanding, and her non-supportiveness of what a lesbian of colour's experiences and reality is in a society that is racist, classist and of course, homophobic. This woman wanted her lover to follow the politically correct line as to how to live her life, as set down largely by white middle class lesbians.

This woman then went on to ask me what it was like to be a lesbian in Toronto. She did not ask me what it was like to be an East Indian lesbian in Toronto. Obviously race is not an issue with her. She assumes that as lesbians we all experience the same sort of problems. She was oblivious as to how race can be an issue....

Joanne: I know, the whole thing is really totally fucked. I mean it's even hard for us to come out to each other for fear of the consequences. I remember one night I went to this gay club in Toronto and there were a few black women in there and I really wanted to go up and speak to them. And it was really difficult. The first thing that came to my mind was: I wonder if they want to be invisible? I mean, do they want me to talk to them? Do they want to be recognised as lesbians by another black woman/lesbian?

Pramila: I think that it's okay in a bar - it's a safe environment. But if you were to meet them on the street another time, or in a restaurant they would probably be a lot more reluctant to talk to you.

Joanne: But I still think that even in a club or bar there is still a fear. You know, like the fear of what might happen if they saw me on the street the next day and I was, say, walking with someone who didn't know I was gay?....

Pramila: I think maybe that some of that tension is a factor of age? My sense is that younger women in this society, in this day and age, are a lot more comfortable, a lot more secure about their sexuality and that maybe it's the older women who feel insecure? That's the sort of impression I get from talking to women in bars.

But, what I think is even more threatening in all of this is that there is a lot of sexual tension when women of the same race meet each other, because I feel it reminds them that they live in so much of a white world and that many of them are involved with lovers who are white, and most times that means that they are culturally separated. But I think that lesbians, period, are all paranoid to some extent or level. Unless they are really out there in the world, their close friends and community know and support them.

Joanne: Which is something we as women of colour don't have - that community support. It's something that we have to begin working on. I don't know how we are going to do it, but I know that I get tired of being invisible to people I work with in the Black community. I know that I'm good in my work and my sexual preference shouldn't be a strike against me.

Pramila: We have to begin a dialogue with other heterosexual women of colour. We have to cross that bridge to create a "new" community.

*   *   *   *   *

SILVER STREAMS

Judith Pilowsky-Santos

They are coming again. I hear the thudding of distant steps coming to the door. I stay motionless, listening. I cannot be sure if it is them or just the metallic daggers of rain, patiently tapping on the roof, forming silver streams, mad streams: running, toward the freedom of the sea.

The noise is still there. What is it? Them or the rats? Grinding their teeth, hungry, savouring the smell of blood, scratching in the ever dark corridors.

I don't know how long I have been in this position. I don't want to move. It hurts, my kidneys ache, pushed against my ribs. It hurts. The wet towels did a good job on me.

I want to urinate. I am afraid of standing up and going to the corner of the room, better I pee here, on the floor where I am lying down, my vagina burns when I pee. It feels better when the warm urine runs down my legs. Luckily the room is dark and I do not see if the urine has blood.

My eyes are accustomed to the darkness enshrouding the room. The other prisoners are sleeping. They moan, but nobody cries. After the interrogations the eyes turn arid, deserted by tears. To cry is to fight, still, for being human. Here, in the prison we are only nightmares, swollen faces, beaten bodies, silhouettes without shadows. Forgotten women. Furrows of dried tears.

The door. Still closed. For how long? Outside the drops of rain give rhythm to the night. Here there are no clocks. Only echoes of steps coming to the door. I am going to try to sleep. To forget the hooded faces. The steps are coming to get me, coming slowly to the door of the room. To forget the lips that I do not see, asking, accusing me. Thousands of questions lurk in the dark corners, sucking up all the air, hammering my head: "Where are the weapons?" - subversive books. Political plots. Against the regime. "Answer us, answer us," the executioners scream. "Answer me," chants the wet towel beating on my back, stabbing my back, one, ten, many times.

I have to think to concentrate. If they open the door and they come for me I have to be prepared. In the interrogation they always try to confuse me. They try to make me say things that are not true. They repeat the same question many times, until I do not know what to answer, until the words have no sense at all after repeating them so often.

The door will open and they will call one of us. Me? Is it my turn again? If only I could remember how long I have been lying here.

A noise. I heard a noise. Is it here inside the room? It is number five, she hands me a piece of bread. I think I was being interrogated when they brought the food. Number five kept a piece of bread for me. But did not keep me any water. The new one, who came three days ago almost died. Was she tortured too much? When they brought the new number to the room, the others gave it my water.

I heard a murmur. Somebody is praying. I try to understand what the voice is saying; I do not listen to the sound of the boots coming to the door....I try to listen to the voice, carefully now "EVERY HEART"....It is not a prayer; it's a song. Somebody is singing. The voice wraps around me...I feel like crying "HAS A RIGHT" ...a song! I am listening to a song! "TO ITS FREEDOM"....

Outside the raining stops. Number five tells me to sleep. She says my turn is not yet. She says that I was the last one to cross the door back to the room. I cannot remember how long ago they interrogated me. I think I fainted. They made me take all my clothes off. The tied electric cables on my toes, on my armpits. In my vagina. The voices accused me, asked me many things, blamed me for atrocities I never committed. In the room. Now. Somebody sings and the words mix with the scratching of the rats, outside, waiting to come in, scurrying down the corridor, slowly coming to open the door. But here in the room. Somebody sings.

Black Women's Studies in Teaching Related to Women: Help or Hindrance to Universal Sisterhood?

Until all of Us Have Made It, None of Us Has Made It.

- Rosemary Brown

Esmeralda Thornhill

Stephanie Martin

Marie-Joseph-Angélique![1] Queen Yaa-Asantewaa![2] Mary Ann Shadd![3] Thanadelthur![4] Queen Nefertiti![5] Harriet Tubman![6]

Are you familiar with these outstanding women of colour? How many instructors in teaching related to women have used or do use them as positive models? How many students of Women's Studies can identify with these pioneers of colour who have marked milestones in the history of woman and humankind? Have their names become common catchwords in an institute of learning such as Simone de Beauvoir?[7]

In 1943, the remarkable Canadian feminist Nellie McClung affirmed that "people must know the past to understand the present and to face the future."[8] Women of colour have played out key roles, have blazed important trails, and have laid down bridges on which many of us today intrepidly tread. Yet much of today's Teaching related to Women - all to its detriment - ignores, omits, or simply fails to acknowledge such realities. For Women's Studies, or Teaching related to Women, by receiving a booster shot in the arm from the Women's Movement, have thus inherited all its accompanying concepts, norms, and...alas, *colour-blindness.*

Drawing so heavily on a social movement which, in itself, tended at the best of times to exclude women of colour, and at the worst of times, to tack them on as an afterthought, present Teaching related to Women still reflects these same exclusionary traits. What has been concretized as Women's Studies, and has come to be known as traditional Women's Studies, fails to bear up well under close scrutiny when it comes to Black Women and other Women of colour. We remain invisible. Nevertheless we Black Women *ARE* indeed Women. We, ourselves, are very much aware of our status as Women and indeed we *DO* concur with the ideas and precepts of the Women's Movement. However, living as we do in a world that persists in seeing us first and foremost as Black, we cannot negate our Blackness. Since "Blackness" is a condition that was and is foisted upon us by an oppressive society, we are therefore inevitably forced to acknowledge this condition, if only for reasons of mere survival. Therefore, we are first and foremost Black, and then Women.

But why talk about Black Women's Studies? What is Black Women's Studies? Interestingly enough, ideologically, we all now seem to be able to grasp and understand fairly well the concept of Black Studies. The need exists for Black Studies programs because, in the final analysis, our curriculum - both visible and hidden - is in fact nothing but a White Studies Program, projecting an image of the world as being a world of Whites that bars Blacks.[9] In the same manner, a terrible need exists for Black Women's Studies because our present Women's Studies and Teaching related to Women programs clearly exclude - especially in their philosophical under-pinnings - Women of colour. In other words, Black Women's Studies is a positive response to the neglect of Black Women by Teaching related to Women.

One fundamental tenet must be kept in mind: Education's basic work is to provoke change.[10] Modified behaviour becomes therefore, an important goal of Teaching related to Women. And thus, Women's Studies, a new field in itself, is nothing if not a catalyst for social change. Women's Studies aspires to complete and correct the record by grafting onto present knowledge, knowledge about women. And so, Teaching related to Women is, *ipso facto*, a progressive social movement. This movement is the fruit of two important social movements: the Black Consciousness Movement and the Women's Liberation Movement. And as such, it behooves Women's Studies to manifest innovation as well as a deep commitment to break with traditional approaches, traditional content, and traditional values. Any Teaching related to Women owes it to itself to go *beyond* the proverbial "cosmetic" cover-up or lip service that tradition Teaching has instituted. Feminist writer Frances Wilson has said that, "Resources for Women's Studies courses in Canada ought to be drawn largely from the history, literature, traditions and social structure of Canada."[11] But I further maintain that we are obliged to assess critically and reevaluate these very sources in order to avoid perpetuating oppressive mechanisms and structures, whether we do this consciously or unconsciously. For, if Women's Studies merely signify that White Women are fighting for the right to be able to oppress Black Women equally with White men, then it makes little sense for Black Women to participate in this struggle, since it is a known fact that to Black Women, oppression by White males or White females makes absolutely no difference - it is the oppression that hurts![12]

Through a progressive social movement like Women's Studies and Teaching related to Women, Sisterhood can become a real worldwide possibility[13] However, to make this a reality, Women's Studies cannot afford the luxury of being shortsighted, tunnel-visioned, or colour-blind. The struggle for equality of Women must be waged not only within the ranks of the fight against sexism, but also on the broader field of the war on racism. If we really mean Women with a capital "W", Women's Studies cannot refuse to perceive colour or difference. Indeed, Women's Studies dare not see everybody only as "women" - professing colour blindness. Real Teaching related to Women dare not continue to deny that there are differences, maintaining that "We are all Women!" or, "We are all human beings!" We *ARE* Women....*YES*! But as Black Women, we have a great deal of cultural, historical, and experiential differences that need to be recognized, acknowledged and shared.

Black Women already share a past far different from that of White Women. Black Women have had a long history of "non-traditional" roles.[14] When White Women were into consciousness-raising sessions, trying to come to grips with who they were quite apart from their husbands and children, Black Women were seeking groups that *could* and *would* address the issues of massive unemployment and underemployment among Black people in general, and Black Women in particular.[15] Today, when Women from the *developed* countries are lobbying for the right to use their maiden name, Women from the *"underdeveloped"* and *oppressed* countries are scrounging for food and water in order to keep their families alive in a hand to mouth existence. When White Women were trying to find time to write or do research, Black Women were trying to find groups that could and would address the poor education their children were receiving.[16] And now, when Women of the *developed* countries are seeking greater sexual freedom and gratification, Women from the *"underdeveloped"* and *oppressed* countries are fighting for their country and their lives in liberation armies. When White Women were devising strategies for getting out of the house and into the labour force, vast numbers of Black Women were suggesting that they would gladly return home and take care of the home and children if the economic system were not so oppressive to Black Men.[17] (At the same time, We, Black Women, were saying to Black Men that a return to the home did not change our independent nature.)[18] And, today, when Women of the *developed* countries are clamouring for the right to abortion on demand, many Women from the *"underdeveloped"* and *oppressed* countries are crying out for help against enforced sterilisation and the imposition of untested and unsafe medical drugs.[19]

In other words, even though multiple issues for Women the World over are truly common denominators, the point remains that it is the *order of priorities* that differs. It is for this precise reason that Teaching related to Women, Women's Studies, and the Women's Movement, must begin to address seriously *issues of economic and racial oppression* in order to be relevant to Black Women and other Women of colour.[20]

Black Women's Studies is a necessary component of, and an essential dimension to, any Teaching related to Women. It should be omnipresent and ubiquitous, pervading and permeating any Women's Studies program.

From a methodological viewpoint, in order to realize fully a program of Teaching related to Women, I posit that Women's Studies:

1. Can no longer remain *colour-blind* to Black Women, to our experiences, to our accomplishments, contributions, social impact, aspirations and preoccupations.

2. Can no longer subscribe to the *Addendum Syndrome* which at times "footnotes" the Black Woman, and at other times tacks on as an "appendix" information about exceptional Women of colour while the main curriculum content remains White Women's Studies.

3. Can no longer exclude from the *decisional levels* and *blue print stages* the *active involvement of Women of colour, who, themselves, experts, can help to ensure that the orientation and materials selected are the most accurate and authentic representation of their group.*

4. *Can no longer ethically* continue to be accomplices in the "Conspiracy of Silence on Racism." Women's Studies is obliged to make an *up-front commitment against racism.* As such, Women's Studies must give in its curriculum, information about the way in which *DISCRIMINATION* and *RACISM* function in society as social forces.

This first ever international coming together of Women to discuss Teaching and Research related to Women must mean from the outset that we believe that we *share a common* concern, a *common* commitment, and a *common* goal. If Educators in the area of Teaching related to Women or Women's Studies are really the progressive activists and committed professionals that we profess to be, if we consider ourselves true Members of the International Community of the concerned, if we believe that we *ARE* indeed, universally, Sisters in Struggle, then we can do NO LESS than *"Agitate! Agitate! Agitate!"*[21] until Black Women's Studies assumes its rightful place in Teaching related to Women as a help to universal Sisterhood!

This paper was originally presented by Esmeralda Thornhill to the First International Conference on Research and Teaching Related to Women at the Simone de Beauvoir Institute, Concordia University, on July 29, 1982.

Footnotes

1. Marie-Joseph-Angélique: Black Montreal Slave who launched the first documented act of defiance against slavery. Apprehending her imminent sale, Marie-Joseph-Angelique set fire to the residence of her mistress before taking flight. The ensuing conflagration ravaged the city, razing over forty buildings. This defiant slave was later captured, brought to trial, condemned, and publicly executed, hanged before being burnt at the stake.

2. Queen Yaa Asantawaa: Black African Queen, known to her people as Yaa Asantewaa the Great. Although the British invaders nick-named her the Old Terror, this Asanti Queen was the live symbol of hope for Ghana's Akan nation against early British oppression. "The woman who carried a gun and the world of state into battle" fought against the ideas and practices of Christianity which she predicted would be a disorienting and disruptive force in Asanti life.

3. Mary-Ann Shadd: Black educator, abolitionist and lawyer, who published one of Canada's early Black Newspapers the *Provincial Freeman* and has been credited with being the first Woman Editor in Canada.

4. Thanadelthur: Chippewa Indian Woman who served during the 1700's as Peacemaker between her People, the Cree, and the Hudson's Bay Company.

5. Queen Nefertiti: One of the more renowned African Queens, shrewdly appropriated by Europe - but who remains African nonetheless. This wise and creative woman had great influence on her husband Akhenaton with whom she is portrayed as sharing equal status. She also wielded mighty political power.

6. Harriet Tubman: Black slave, abolitionist, feminist, educator, orator - Moses of Her People. Born a slave in the United States, Harriet Tubman fled to the Northern States where she worked, saved her earnings and reentered the South in order to lead her parents and family to safety. This proved to be the first of nineteen trips whereby, in spite of a bounty of $40,000 on her head, Harriet Tubman "conducted" along the Underground Railroad (secret network of places and resource people) more than 300 Black slaves who found freedom in Canada and settled the region of Southern Ontario.

7. Simone de Beauvoir Institute: The Department of Women's Studies and Research on Women of Concordia University, and host to the First International Conference on Teaching and Research related to Women, Montreal, Quebec, July 26 - August 4, 1982.

8. Gwen Matheson, (Editor), *Women in the Canadian Mosaic* (Toronto: Peter Martin Associates Ltd., 1976 "Introduction"), p.IX.

9. Robert Moore, "Race and Education for the 1980's" *Race Relations: New Perspectives, New Delivery Systems for Education.* Proceedings of the Conference on Race Relations and Education, January 28 and 29, 1982 hosted by the Ontario Human Rights Commission, Race Relations Division (Toronto: Ontario Ministry of Labour, 1982), p.35.

10. Frances Wilson. "The New Subject: Women's Studies," *Women in the Canadian Mosaic*, Edited by Gwen Matheson (Toronto: Peter Martin Associates Ltd., 1976), p.195.

11. *Idem,* p.190.

12. Rosemary Brown, "A New Kind of Power," *Women in the Canadian Mosaic*, Edited by Gwen Matheson (Toronto: Peter Martin Associates Ltd., 1976), p.295.

13. *Ibidem.*

14. Frances Rodgers-Rose, *The Black Woman.* Beverley Hills (California: Sage Publications Inc., 1980), p.296

15. *Idem,* p.297

16. *Ibidem.*

17. *Ibidem.*

18. *Ibidem.*

19.   "Human Guinea Pigs," *Afro Can*, May 1982, p.1.

20.   Frances Rodgers-Rose, *op.cit.*, p.297.

21.   *"Agitate! Agitate! Agitate!"*: Famous exhortation of Marcus Mosiah Garvey, founder of the Universal Negro Improvement Association.

Bibliography

Brathwaite, Rella., *The Black Woman.* Toronto: 1975.

Davis, Angela Y., *Women, Race and Class.* New York: Random House, 1981.

Karenga, Maulana., *Kawaida Theory: An Introductory Outline.* Inglewood California: Kawaida Publications, 1980.

Malcolm X., *By Any Means Necessary.* New York: Pathfinder Press, 1980.

Matheson, Gwen., (Editor). *Women in the Canadian Mosaic.* Toronto: Peter Martin Associates Ltd., 1976.

Moore Robert. "Race and education for the 1980's." *Race Relations: New Perspectives, New Delivery Systems for Education.* Proceedings of the Conference on Race Relations and Educations. January 28 and 29, 1982. Hosted by the Ontario Human Rights Commission, Race Relations Division, Toronto: Ontario Ministry of Labour, 1982.

Reunion A Mexico., Conference mondiale de l'Annee internationale de la femme, Mexico, 19 juin-29 juillet 1975. New York: Nations Unies, 1975.

Rodgers-Rose, La Frances., (Editor). *The Black Woman.* Beverley Hills California: Sage Publications Inc., 1980, p.296

Rodney, Walter., *How Europe Underdeveloped Africa.* Washington, D.C.: Howard University Press, 1974.

Thornhill, Esmeralda., *Race and Class in Canada: The Case of Blacks in Quebec.* Paper presented to the National Council for Black Studies V Annual Conference, Academic Excellence and Social Responsibility: Science and Politics in Black Studies. Chicago, March 17-20, 1982.

Williamson, Jane., *New Feminist Scholarship: A Guide to Bibliographies.* Old Westbury, New York: The Feminist Press, 1979.

A Poem by **Ayanna Black**

in memory of lorraine

she sent to sleep with the moon

but

she did not rise

she was found by her lover

with rose pricklings on her arm

my soliloquy was

why?

she seemed to blossom

i recall a voice inside me saying

a rose blossoming in winter

could it be cultured?

IMAGES OF BLACK WOMEN

By **Claire Preito** and **Roger McTair**

These photographs were taken between the years 1974-1976 by Claire Preito and Roger McTair. They are images of just a few of the Black women who were active in different areas and organizations in Toronto during those years.

Ruby Campbell and Makeda Silvera in the front lines at the African Liberation Day march 1975.

Marlene Green—political activist talks with a friend at a Black Education Project Family Day in 1976.

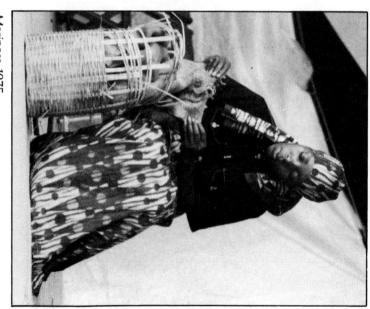

Mariposa 1975.

Black Women's Organization Picnic, 1974.

After shopping Saturday afternoon in 1974.

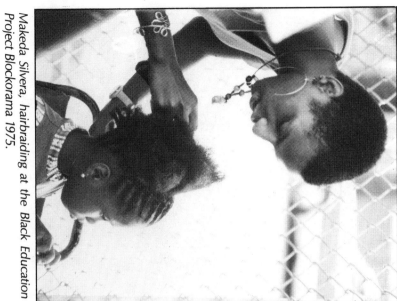

Makeda Silvera, hairbraiding at the Black Education Project Blockorama 1975.

Lucina Thomas—dancer with Afro-Caribbean Theatre performs at "Mariposa" 1975.

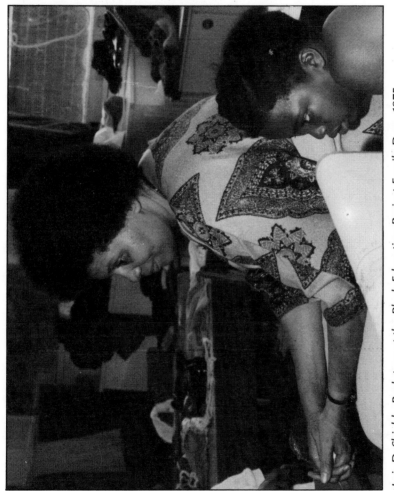

Lois DeShield—Backstage at the Black Education Project Family Day—1975.

Meena Dhar

A Short Story

Anita Gore

It was not always like this. When I first came to Indore, I used not to wake up exhausted, walk exhausted, sleep exhausted. For more than an hour I have been lying in bed. Already I am half an hour late for work. The children in my class will be whimpering 'I want my teacher.' The other teachers will say 'Perhaps Keerti is not well today. She has been looking so tired this week.'

I find it hard to believe that I have come to be known as one who is prone to not being well.

'Perhaps you have a vitamin deficiency,' my mother said when she came to see me a month ago. 'Perhaps,' I said. And she bought me bottles and bottles of vitamin tablets. For a month now, I have been taking them every day. If I had thought of it, I could have told my mother, even a month ago, that vitamins weren't my problem. But I don't think of much these days.

Yes. I know what my problem is. I have started to live with a sense of resignation.

* * * * *

Sometimes I feel surprised that what has happened now, did not happen before. Surprised at the energy that must have been mine.

As I remember it, 'the struggle' began with my first attempt at being an ordinary person. It was in my last year of high school that my parents finally agreed that I was old enough to opt out of the school bus if I so chose. Old enough to ride the city's transport service.

* * * * *

I live twenty miles away from downtown, where my school is. It will be an hour's ride in a double decker. And I am excited, yearning towards adulthood, towards feeling part of the city.

After riding the double decker for a week, I no longer enjoy the actual ride. I am still excited by the image of me as an adult person. I see myself waking up in the mornings to walk into the big city. I buy a newspaper on the way to the bus stop, to reinforce my image, to calm the dread in my chest.

More men than women travel on the bus. More often than not, a man sits next to me. And too often, I feel him edging closer, feel his elbow in my ribs or his legs rubbing against mine. I want to be reading my newspaper, or looking out onto the city. Instead I am preoccupied. With anger for the bastard who's imposing himself on me.

'So I hear you take the public bus into school now,' says my aunt to me on the weekend.

'Yes,' I say matter of factly.

'Do you prefer it to the school bus?'

'Yes. I kind of like riding with office people, rather than school kids. I like reading the newspaper like everyone else on the bus. I guess I'm just a healthy adolescent wanting to be an adult.' And I laugh self-consciously. But I will not admit that rather than reading my paper and being adult-like, I am often preoccupied with the man sitting next to me, edging closer. I will not admit to my 'woman-like' problems. Woman-like is not my image of adult.

I don't know how to deal with the men on the bus. If I get engrossed in the newspaper, I think, the prick beside me will be affected by my non-sexual vibes. I can be in control, I try to believe: I cannot be imposed upon.

I find I become more sensitive with time. Waves of anger begin to overtake my rational, my 'adult self.' Sometimes I am not sure if the man touched me by accident before I feel myself in rage.

Then one day it starts. My hitting back. The elbow that was digging into my stomach has become a hand on my thigh. My anger has been rising. Even in my rage, I am somewhat frightened. Of an unimaginable situation that I could create. Cool down, cool down I am saying to myself. But before I know it, I am kicking, hard, at the feet beside me. And shouting. And now my fear is as large as my anger. I am shouting at a respectable, middle-aged man. Suddenly I stop. I make my way down the stairs, into the lower deck. As I walk, I hear the upper deck burst into tittering laughter. At this school girl, already insane.

But I will not resign myself to the school bus. I ride the double decker, sometimes standing, sometimes fuming all the way, occasionally the mad school girl in the bus, sometimes relieved at having a woman sit next to me, sometimes sure that my mind power is beginning to work and it is that that is keeping the man beside me on his side of the seat.

* * * * *

Two years later, at nineteen, I have convinced my parents that I am old enough to spend the money I have saved on travelling. I have spent considerable time during the last two years hanging around Bombay's 'Rex Hotel,' the hippies' residence. I am almost infatuated with hippie culture, its ideals of freedom and the rejecting of social norms - perhaps because I find the norms for me, as an Indian woman, rather distasteful. The norm for me would be to continue to stay at home while going to university, and then, upon graduation, to get married.

My parents have agreed that I am old enough to make my own decisions. But they are afraid for me. They know of no girl who travels alone. What of Jane, I say. (Jane is the daughter of American friends of theirs who visited us en route to Goa). Jane, they say, is American. White people are seen as being in a class of their own. But you, an Indian woman on your own, no one will know how to see you.

Despite my experiences travelling on Bombay's transit system alone, I myself am only slightly nervous about travelling across the country. Because I am so eager to step out into the hippie route, to save myself from the probabilities of my future. And also, making me feel more secure is the knowledge that there is almost a hippie path through the country. A couple of hotels in each town where the hippies live. I am counting on staying in these, where most men are hippies and, I have found, unthreatening to me.

I will go first to Manali I decide. It's a town in the Himalayan range. A hippie paradise, I have heard.

My bus gets into Manali late at night. I find my way to 'The Hill View,' a name that has been mentioned to me at Bombay's Rex.

There is a woman at the desk. The cheapest accommodation available, she tells me, is a bed in a dormitory. Only two rupees a night. How does she see me, I'm wondering, when she asks to see my passport. I don't have a passport, I'm Indian I say in Hindi. I'm a student in Bombay, on vacation. We have summer holidays... I spill out words and words, nervous of being seen as a whore, trying to create a non-whore-Indian-woman-travelling-alone image for her. Quick. Before, in an attempt to deal with an unfamiliar situation, she grabs the whore image that she is probably familiar with.

'Do you have a dormitory for women only?' I ask her, half in an attempt to convince her that I'm not looking to pick up men. In my near panic, I'm not very perceptive of what impression I'm making on her; I still don't know how she sees me when she picks up a flashlight and is ready to show me to a room. We go into a dormitory and she lights up an empty bed.

'There is a woman next to you,' she says, 'but there are some men in this room, though only foreigners.'

'That's fine,' I say in relief. She must see me as something other than a whore if she said that.

My first night alone in a hotel. I could find the washroom, brush my teeth, wash my face. But I am so excited, I just want to lie down and feel the excitement, the warmth in my stomach. I pull out my sleeping bag, take off my pants and crawl in.

'You're Indian, aren't you?' whispers a woman's voice on my right. Sleeping next to a hippie woman in Manali. I feel warmth lick the inside of my chest.

'Yep,' I say, knowing that I'm something of a novelty. And then, modestly trying to steer away from my novelty-ness, I say 'What is this room like in the day?'

'It's okay. There are four white boys, two white girls including me and now one brown girl. Which of these will be here tomorrow, I don't know. They are nice enough, these dormitories, though I wouldn't mind living in one for women only.'

'Hmm. I don't know,' I say.

'Why? Do you like to pick up white boys in dormitories?'

I'm surprised. Most westerners I've known have been unsure of what my values as an Indian woman are likely to be, most have been polite, cautious. I'm usually glad for this, partly because I'm trying to enter this new community, and am unsure of norms, and politeness seems safe. But her smartass-ness is now making me all quivery inside with giggles. However, I'm too shy or stiff or something to giggle yet.

'Well, I don't know. I kind of like a balanced atmosphere,' I say stupidly.

'To be honest, I haven't noticed a great deal of balance between men and women. Have you?'

I'm not sure of what she's saying. Is this feminist talk, or is she saying that there is no balance because women are stupid, or what? I don't know where what I say next comes from. Perhaps simply from wanting to shock myself out of being too shy or too stupid to be anything other than stiff, perhaps from the frustration of feeling so new to everything. I don't know from where and with what relevance to what has been said before, but what I say now is, 'Are you lesbian?' And then as inexplicably, I fall asleep.

The next day, I am sitting in a restaurant when Alice comes in, sees me and comes up to my table.

'I saw your sleeping face this morning. But you haven't seen me. Do you recognize my voice?'

'Yep. And I know what your name is too. I saw it written on your knapsack this morning. I'm Keerti.'

'It's a nice enough hotel we're in, Keerti. But this morning I saw a lovely little cottage up above old Manali village, just below where the forest starts, above a loud gushing stream. And only sixty rupees a month. I'm thinking of moving up there, and it'll save me money if I find someone to share it with. You wouldn't be interested, would you? Oh, but before you answer, I should repeat what I don't think you heard last night...'

And she bursts into laughter and then continues with mock seriousness 'My dear, I must confess that I have had lesbian experiences...'

We both laugh.

I'm watching myself. Thinking of licking her crotch. Yech. All so gooey and soft and womanlike it would be. I want to be associated with toughness. My own gooey, soft vagina doesn't seem to be mine. I have to be twice as tough, twice as precise to make up for it. My body is firm. Tense muscles running down my back, my legs. But in between my tight muscles is this unknown area that turns all yecky, swampy sometimes.

A week after I've been living with her, one would think that I was sensually obsessed with her. For two nights I pull my sleeping bag into the next room, on the excuse of not wanting to sleep in the same room as the fire. I'm edgy. My dreams hover around the theme of her misunderstanding me, of her thinking that I want sex with her.

Suddenly, I confront myself. Would it be a misunderstanding? I do want a right out there man, not a hidden swampy woman. But still, I seem to be yearning, maybe not so much for sex, but to hold her. Hold her and lick her clean ears.

Slowly I began to touch her. Would wake finding my arms around her, would sleep hugging her all night. She, I think, was being careful not to make the first moves, to let me move at my pace.

Slowly, the picture in my mind of the yecky swamp between her legs became a memory. The swamp was maybe still out there, between other women's legs. Between her legs and mine was this precious area, sometimes soft, fig-like, stretching. Sometimes muscular, clasping spasmodically, holding firm my finger.

Now and then, the swamp would return, as it still does. On cloudy, lost days, sometimes in dreams of figs getting overripe, mushy, putrid. Sometimes after reading of men's voices talking of the jelly on women's chests, the holes between their legs.

In India, in general, I don't think women are yecky. They are forever giving, forever modest, forever female. If they are good. If they are bad, they are whores. I don't think Indians see yeck between women's legs. I don't know how I came to see it. Through rock music maybe, or books, or my western friends. These same things perhaps, gave me images of women who were neither forever only female nor whores.

* * * * *

After a month in Manali, Alice and I travelled to Delhi. There she saw the fury that lived inside the calm, happy Indian woman she had known.

I remember travelling with her in a crowded bus in Delhi at rush hour. There were only a few seats left, and I had found one way at the back of the bus, she somewhere in the middle. Soon the aisles were full of standees. A man was standing next to me and it was not long before he was pushing his erection into my shoulder. I made an attempt to be above these hassles by doing arithmetic divisions in my head. The pushing had turned to a rub. He was snickering to his friend. I will be calm, I will be calm I repeat to myself. The next thing I know, I'm standing up. I've punched his face. I'm screaming. Laughter at the mad woman in the bus. I've been through this too many times before I think to myself in a low tide of my anger. Then the high tide is upon me again. 'ALICE COME ON, LET'S GET OFF THIS FUCKING BUS,' I shout. Somehow where there was no room at all, there is a passage to let the mad woman pass to the front. Alice is behind me. 'YOU GODDAMM FUCKERS,' I scream in English. Anger is hardly something for a woman of my culture to display. I take refuge in western culture when I feel that mine would surely choke me, take refuge in mine when the west's picture of the dirty, lazy cunt gets too strong.

I'm off the bus. Unable to look at Alice, to let my mad face be seen. I'm stomping into the ground, raising red dust around my feet. We walk in the sun for an hour into Connaught Place, Delhi's downtown.

'Why do you not accept your anger? You have a right to be angry,' said Alice to me after witnessing a number of instances of the contradiction of my fury and my shame of it. Shame for being so small-minded, so anger-preoccupied.

Accept my anger? Already I think I am being made almost one-dimensioned, made shallow by it. I am afraid that one day, it will swallow me, that there will be nothing left of me other than a block of anger.

That summer I juggled anger and alternately shame, with humour that I was developing as a result of Alice's mimicry of the man who pinched her ass as he was walking past, or the man who sat next to me on the bus and pressed closer and closer until I was nearly off the seat. I was building images of their silliness and absurdity that I sometimes managed to throw them into before rage hit me, evading anger with laughter.

* * * * *

That was the summer four years ago. The next four years, the years before I came to Indore, I spent at Delhi's university. For the most part, I spent my time within the campus, where most men were classmates who may bother other women on the streets, but left us alone.

* * * * *

Now here in Indore, I remember I used to turn anger into laughter. Perhaps I could turn resignation into laughter. But a sub-culture of images, jokes cannot be built alone, in isolation. I do not think that I am isolated because this culture makes limp beings of all women, and my co-teachers have simply started taking their limpness for granted. No, I don't think that we have lifelessness in common.

To begin with, I wore pants to work. But soon, the principal spoke to me. Yes, I know, she said, in Delhi and Bombay, pants are acceptable. But here, they are not. And as a teacher. you are always under inspection. Parents worry about the influences on their children.

I started to wear a sari. Now, to all, I looked like a teacher. I was presumed to be a teacher. It is not that a teacher's life is empty. It is full, but filled mainly with thoughts of the children she teaches, of her work. She wears a sari to show her serious-mindedness. If she is not married, there is no man who she can be seen with, and since women do not go out by themselves at night, it is only on the weekend that she may perhaps take time off from her thoughts of work, may perhaps see a movie with her girl friends during the day.

The women I work with, I don't find lifeless. They are women who find room for themselves within the powerful stereotype of a female teacher. There are those who are keenly interested in the children's different personalities, those who read extensively on new methods of teaching that they experiment with in their own classrooms, that they help others incorporate.

But I still want to be a common person, with my job as one of my interests. I feel sapped of my personhood, and find that I'm not wanting or not able to substitute the female teacher's personality for the common person I always wanted to be.

Two Poems by Dee September

Descending the Veld

The night has left a taste
of grief and salt in my mouth
my eyes are two black holes
seeping into burnt thunder

memory of you comes flying
through the swish of blades
the rat-ta-tat of guns
and the wounded sound of drums

like smoke in the drizzle
you come out of the wet night
branding your echoing laughter
into the swelling ache of my heart

pain is the corner of sorrow
in a silence far more brutal
than the splintering of speech
sorrow is the curtain of endurance

it is only soft candle light
that can melt these angry tears
or the sharp hammering of sunlight
that will explode through the darkness

speaking in a language of calm
i am left holding joy in a clenched fist
following your shadow and footsteps
on the long journey homeward bound

Children Of My Country

In my country
children are born old
with the taste of fear
in their famished mouths

Children are born old
with eyes staring - betrayed
by an insane world
exploding with the shock of war

Children are born old
knowing hunger pains
and violent death
before the age of life

In my country
children are not innocent babes
for a moment longer than
the blink of any eye

For time more than
a split second that it takes
children are born old
before their innocence can survive

Post Patriation: The Antithesis of Termination to Special Status of the Aboriginal Peoples

The following is a copy of the Brief Presentation to Sub-Committee on Sex Discrimination Against Indian Women to the Standing Committee on Indian Affairs and Northern Development, prepared and presented by the **Ontario Native Women's Association** on January 19, 1983.

Since 1972, the Ontario Native Women's Association has been in existence. Starting from six organized groups in the province of Ontario, this organization now represents 36 Anishinabequek chapters and speaks on behalf of all Native women in the province. Our membership lives in rural, isolated, unorganized communities, towns, reserves and urban centres. A large percentage of our constituents are Status, on and off reserve, Non-Status and Metis.

The logo for the Ontario Native Women's Association speaks for itself: O - our home is first; N - Native women speak; W - working together; A - assisting our own. The provincial organization serves as a co-ordinating body to address the many socio-economic, cultural, recreational and political issues facing our Native communities, in particular, those issues specifically identifiable to Native women and our children. It has been one of the Ontario Native Women's Associations' objectives to create a forum through which Native women can speak collectively as a unified voice in Ontario.

However, before this could happen, the Ontario Native Women's Association had the responsibility of making Native women in Ontario aware of the many issues affecting them and their family members - namely, the existing legislations, both provincial and federal.

Hence, the Ontario Native Women's Association proceeded to have leadership and awareness workshops, followed by research efforts to bring focus on legislation, the Indian Act, in particular, to the attention of our Native women. Through this effort, Native women in Ontario have become increasingly politically aware of the current issues facing our people today. We have recognized that we have a valuable contribution to make to address the political developments on issues facing Native people.

In March, 1982, Native women of Ontario gathered together to discuss the future of Native women. At the end of the conference it was confirmed that Native women in Ontario do not recognize the "legal definitions" used by the Government of Canada to divide our people. The delegates to this conference had confirmed the meaning of the word, "Aboriginal" to be descendants of the first people of this land who are presently Status, Non-Status, Metis and Inuit. This definition provides that the Aboriginal peoples of this land be treated as equals among their number and kind.

To be more specific, the Native women have expressed concern that the current legal definition which appears in the present *Indian Act* would be used to determine who is and who is not an Indian. If this definition of Indian is used, then some 500,000 Native women in Canada would be affected by such a decision. Where then, would the Non-Status Indians and children fit? Who then, is to protect and safeguard their rights? It is for this reason that the word "Indian" as specified in the *Canadian Constitution Act 1981* warrants further negotiations among our own people first; then to the appropriate governments. It is for these reasons that the current definition of "Indian" cannot be supported or endorsed by this organization.

With the patriation of the *Canadian Constitution Act 1981* in April 1982, Canada's constitution now joins together Indian, Inuit, and Metis into one general category of "Aboriginal Peoples." It would appear that the trend by the federal government is to favour policies and programs that reflect the issue of the Aboriginal peoples as a whole. It all sounds good; however, what is at stake is the resolution of the identification of and definition of the Aboriginal and Treaty rights which includes among other things: the moral, political and legal question of membership, legal status, financial implications and powers. The new constitution requires that the issue of "rights" be resolved at the meeting of the First Ministers' conference this spring (1983).

It is also recognized that the word "existing" was placed into the Canadian *Constitution Act 1981* to expedite the patriation process. It was observed by the Native women that the entrenchment of Aboriginal and Treaty rights was sacrificed by the Government of Canada to reach a constitutional accord with the provinces. As well, there is no guarantee that the political and legal rights presently articulated by our Aboriginal leaders will be considered. As a result, the Ontario Native Women's Association has taken a firm position that the primary issue of Aboriginal and Treaty rights must be resolved first before any changes in legislation and policies related specifically to Aboriginal people occur. This special constitutional position of Aboriginal peoples of this land must be reflected in any changes to legislation, policies and programs.

With the signing of the Canadian Constitution Act on April 17, 1982, our organization, along with the other Aboriginal organizations, have begun the slow process of defining and negotiating our internal organizations' positions. This process is deemed important since it is the time to enter into hard negotiations about what rights are to be confirmed and entrenched. Moreover, there must be a period of time for Native women to resolve and negotiate the agenda item first. Governments must realize that we are talking about our constitutional rights and therefore, have far-reaching effects than merely something to put down on paper, to be easily discarded or dissembled. To say the least, this important process has not been given the opportunity to be fully realized.

What we have now is a separate process which focuses narrowly upon one issue: the *Indian Act* and the Indian women. It is duly recognized that the *Indian Act* has openly discriminated against Aboriginal women for hundreds of years; that the Canadian Constitution prohibits such type of discrimination; that the issue of discrimination must be resolved within the next three years as specified in the Charter of Rights; that the Government of Canada has been receiving political pressure from international, national, and regional quarters; that the Native women in Ontario have resolved that all discriminatory sections in the *Indian Act* be immediately stricken down; and that the rights be restored to those individuals who have lost it. However, for whatever factors are articulated, it becomes our responsibility to issue caution that the

It is duly recognized that the Indian Act *has openly discriminated against Aboriginal women for hundreds of years.*

issue of discrimination in the *Indian Act* must be resolved in a manner that does derogate or abrogate the Aboriginal and Treaty rights. The whole question of discrimination of the *Indian Act* must be viewed from a holistic view in relationship to the Aboriginal and Treaty rights entrenchment.

We see that the abolition of section 12(1)(b) from the *Indian Act*, as it exists now, would not affect the present negotiating process taking place between the Aboriginal peoples (including Native women) of this land and the Government of Canada in resolving the issue of Aboriginal and Treaty rights. Further to this point, the *Indian Act* is only an administrative tool and can be changed to end the discriminatory clauses against Native women.

Over the years, Native women have expressed repeatedly that there should be attempts to involve them in the direct consultation and negotiation phases on the very issues that directly affect them. The Indian women and the *Indian Act* is such an issue. The changes must come from the people themselves, not dictated by government. Communities - both rural and urban, including reserves - must be given the courtesy of consultation and negotiation prior to the making of government legislation and policy. Ontario Native women believe that there should be extensive consultation with the various segments of the Native communities on any proposed changes and discussions on the *Indian Act* by the Government of Canada. It has been generally found that only until Aboriginal people "personalize" the very laws that determine their lives, does the law mean anything to them. By the same token, Aboriginal women feel that there must be general agreement among Aboriginal people as to the nature of amendments to be made in order to rectify the situation.

A futile attempt by the Federal government has been made to consult and negotiate with the various segments of the Native communities across Canada. Our question then becomes, why the urgency and the secrecy about an issue that is so political and diversified as this one?

In retrospect to my statements made so far, we cannot emphasize enough, the caution to proceed with the resolution of the issue of discrimination in the *Indian Act* without looking at the broader context in relation to the Aboriginal and Treaty rights issue.

Should the thrust for changes occur prior to the resolution of the Aboriginal and Treaty rights issue; then the constitution wording is really a mandate for the government through its courts to begin a rapid dismantling of all special legal and jurisdictional arrangements affecting Aboriginal people. Hence, the only possible conclusion is that the 1969 White Paper policy was never shelved - but has re-emerged through a culmination of 13 years of preparatory time by the Federal government to do away with the special status of the Aboriginal peoples.

In view of the fact that the Standing Committee on Indian Affairs and Northern Development has received instructions from the House of Commons to study the provisions of the *Indian Act* dealing with the membership and Indian Status issues; we shall now focus the balance of our remarks on the predominant issue of the *Indian Act*, which is just as equally valid and equally important to us as Native women, as heads of Native families.

Aboriginal women remain united in the convictions that "INDIAN IDENTITY" must be preserved and the most valuable role we have is to ensure survival of this identity for future generations. Women know that economic self sufficiency is the foundation for individuals and groups of individuals. For the most part, people can no longer exist without a viable economic foundation. Traditional native ways to provide food and sustenance has been slowly eroded - by treaties, urbanization, corporate economic development, government intervention, and resource management of wild life and fish. With few exceptions, Native people no longer have a choice to live by the traditional ways. They have been coerced, manipulated and persuaded to adapt to other means of economic maintenance. The women surveyed in 1980 believe that in adapting and adjusting to the Canadian economic system, their identity must not be compromised in the process.

A researcher's thoughts about the research undertaken in 1980 by the Ontario Native Women's Association stated: "To begin with, I must say that through Ontario Native Women's Association and their research work, I have been made aware of Indian people and their problems, problems that before had never occurred to me. I have found that through the interviews that I, like most Native women, had never heard of the *Indian Act*, much less, just what it entailed. I was not aware that Indian people regardless of their

Over the years, Native women have expressed repeatedly that there should be attempts to involve them in...the very issues that directly affect them. The Indian women and the Indian Act *is such an issue*

Native ancestry were placed in categories - Status, Non-Status, or Metis and were either Indian or non-Indian according to the *Indian Act*. Being in the category, Metis, did not hold any meaning to me until I learned that Metis people were not considered to be Indians under the present *Indian Act* in regards to Treaty rights and benefits. I truly believe that regardless of my label, I am still an Indian."[1]

[1]O.N.W.A. - *A Perspective*, 1980

When one speaks on Indian identity, one is speaking about being a member of a nation, whether it is the Cree, Ojibway, Mohawk or Iroquois. The Metis, along with the other nations, have their distinctive cultural and ancestral heritage. It becomes important, then, that the membership sections contained in the *Indian Act* be reviewed and changed by Native people. It was felt that non-Natives, including Parliament, have no right to determine Indian identity, Indian status and Indian membership.

The following scenario is the general trend of thought by the Native women in Ontario on the many suggested proposals to change the *Indian Act*. Native women feel strongly about:

1. special status and rights be recognized by the Government of Canada;
2. that Native women should not lose their status upon marriage to a non-Indian;
3. that non-Indian women marrying a status Indian man should not gain status;
4. Native women who lost their status upon marriage should be given their legal rights back and the restoration of these rights be retroactive to the day rights were lost;
5. band membership should be determined by Aboriginal people themselves;

6. an appeal type protection be established and available to pro-
    vide for checks and balances on errors of human judgement;
7. the membership issue must be resolved before the government
    can take action on band powers.

Regarding the question of non-Indian rights in the *Indian Act*, this
issue warrants further discussion and analysis. The issue of
residency, political and legal rights, retention of rights upon death
or divorce from registered Indian remains unresolved. The whole
question must be reviewed in more detail

With respect to the rights of children from such marriages, there
is an overwhelming response that supports the granting of legal
status and rights for children. It is believed that the children of
Indian ancestry and the rights of these children must be protected.

With regard to the double mother clause of the *Indian Act*, it is
believed that these children/youth/adults affected by such laws
should not lose their status at the age of 21.

It is believed that illegitimate children of the registered Indian -
male and female, should have the right to be registered as an Indian
and that right should be retroactive from October 13, 1956.

Indian people who do not appear on the current ban lists and
general lists of the Department of Indian Affairs should be entitled
to be registered as Indians.

Native women do not agree that we should have to transfer band
membership and become a member of the spouse's band membership list. We feel that each spouse should retain his membership
and rights in his own respective bands. The option of allowing the
spouse to join the band of the other is supported. In relationship to
the rights of children, they should be enlisted in the mother's band
list and that they should be given the choice of registered membership in either one of the parent's band lists at the age of majority.

Regarding re-instatement of those individuals who lost their
status Native women through marriage to a non-Indian should apply
for re-instatement. The option of reinstatement period should be
wide open with no cut off date for application for obtaining legal
status. As well, descendants of women who lost their status by
marriage to a non-Indian should gain status whether the woman is
alive or whether she applied for re-instatement. People of non-
Aboriginal descendancy should not have political rights.

Regarding the financial implications involved in this process, Native women believe that the federal government should give additional funds to purchase more land. This will allow the bands to accommodate any influx of reinstated members. For those individuals who lost their status involuntarily these individuals should not have to pay back the band for the per capita share of the capital and revenue monies. However, should these individuals be forced to pay back the per capita share, then the pay back portion should be equivalent to the share paid at the time of loss of status. As well, interest rates should not be applied to band funds over that period of time. In cases where a woman who held a certificate of possession but lost her rights and who had to surrender her home, should be compensated for her loss upon reinstatement. It remains unclear whether bands should claim compensation and repayment of lost annuity payments on behalf of reinstated mothers.

In conclusion, it is very clear that the Aboriginal women who reside in the province of Ontario desire:

- equal rights for both male and female under existing legislation for those of Aboriginal ancestry;
- will insist upon and protect the Aboriginal and Treaty rights, that we as equal members of our respective nations will determine;

and therefore:

- support the immediate removal of the relevant discriminatory sections of the *Indian Act*;
- support, and will seek support from all governing and non-governing bodies, Native and Non-Native, to ensure that the Aboriginal and Treaty rights of our people of today and tomorrow are protected through entrenchment within our own governments and your government.

Mrs. Black, an Indian woman, Missinaibi, Ontario

The Public Archives of Canada

so she could walk

nila gupta

for arvinder

the family came for her   travelled long miles   across oceans   so
that she could walk   from a country   brought to its knees   three
hundred years   of rule by force   and hanging trees   polio of the leg
a simple operation   in three hours   the shine of a blade   and she
limps less   though delicate still   and those here longer than they
say   watch out   these canadian winters   are so dangerous   she
limps less   but walking is a struggle   and   now   it is winter

and the snow falls   and everywhere there are snowballs   and her
brother   is jeered at   and crushed in ice   his turban soaked   and
ripped off   she fears snowfalls   her own fall

and the children moving   like fast glaciers down long halls   floors
glazed like ice   movements like whips   the cracks of ice

and it is winter   when the talk of tans and exotic lands has faded
when the darkest child has already gone to yellowish white   she is
brown   too brown   they say

in history class   they are reading   my india   primitive pagan india
the mutiny of 1857   and she knows differently   bharati raped and
renamed   and nowhere a mention of queen of Jhansi   on horseback
child on her hip   leading her village people   on a defensive-offensive
against the pillagingrapingkillingexploitingwhitemen   she reads the
index   in search of her name

in science class   they talk about melanin   at first   the kids just
snicker   into their breakers   then   in geography class   they see
films   a land   swarming with hungrydiseaseddyingpeople   full of
cripplespotbelliedchildren   and perpetual floods   it is always
monsoon season   and now   a benevolent man   appears   in white
coat   teaches   the underdeveloped   what is good for them
missionary zeal   the kids get to inventing bleach   strong pungent
stuff   they call it perfume   here   they say   try this   it's a gift
she does not smile

she walks   down the halls   class after class   alone   seats herself
with a far-away look   travels long distances with the lowering of her
eyelids   look   you can't touch me   her eyes say   the rows of chair
like teeth   they call her dog   afraid she'll bite   the empty chairs on
each side of her   gaps in the perfect plastic smile

the teachers won't call upon her   to answer their questions
annoyed   at her nasal sounds   in english 101   the eruption of
laughter   she knows   anyways   that the question presupposes the
answer   and is relieved   but one of them   who had seen
much-of-the-world   thinks   not fair   treat-all-of-them-the-same
she is startled   had become so insular   does not answer   they call
her rude   another name   to hurl   hoping to fall her

134

and a man   is pushed   onto the subway tracks   and the train
go home paki   is coming   the young men shout and laugh   the t.v.
screams   a young family   on the elevator up   holds upon the doors
on the 10th floor   to let some adolescents in   who brandish broken
beer bottles   in return   the parents must fall   on their children
to protect them   felled   spray of glass   jagged blades   and
everywhere a stabbing   child developmentalists say   everything is
as it should be   everything is unfolding   according to plan

she blinks back tears   knows she must see clearly   to walk carefully

it is spring   she walks a strong walk   but they are waiting   for her
in the air   they can't smell curry and oil poori and dahl for breakfast
scents they are trained to hate   confusion   like hunting dogs after
prey   enraged   thrown off the scent   by a river   enraged   was
she   trying to pass?

Window-pane

Dora Nipp

"Jun, hurry and put on your shoes. Ba-ba will probably be hungry," ma-ma called from the kitchen. "Quick, quick."

Turning back to the cast-iron pot, she scraped up the last grains of the rice and pressed them into the canister. Atop the steaming mound were sprinkled bits of salted turnip and a few pieces of fish left over from dinner. With the wooden spatula she patted the meat and preserved vegetables so that they sat snugly together, making sure that nothing would spill over. Ma-ma reached for the lid and capped it on. A dish towel was then wrapped around several times to keep the canister warm.

Wiping her hands on her apron, she uttered a softly compelling whisper, "Come, come." As her words were absorbed by the quiet, she glanced up to see Jun. Still trying to shake away the sleep, Jun came toddling down the narrow corridor. Hopping on one foot, he was unable to balance himself as he tried to pull on the remaining shoe. Trailing behind him was a sweater he had grabbed from the bedpost in the room he shared with Fun and Po. It wasn't his. Judging from the size, it most likely belonged to Poi, his second eldest brother. But, no matter. It did its job.

The dead glare of the kitchen light stung Jun's eyes and he had to squint for several seconds before they would stop watering. Minutes before, ma-ma had stealthily crept into the boys' bedroom. Her hands had reached out to summon Jun, but found little Po instead. It was difficult to distinguish the small dark heads when tucked under the heavy quilt. Ma-ma drew breath when she realized her error. She tried again. This time, the stern but gentle touch on his shoulder told Jun he had to get up from the warmth to run an errand for ma-ma.

A yawn escaped.

"Oh my, big enough to catch a fly with," teased his mother.

The boy grinned a slight grin. He pulled the sweater over his head, pushed up the droopy sleeves, and reached out to grasp the rice ma-ma was handing him.

"Go quickly. Don't stay and talk. They have work to do and you must sleep. Tell ba-ba that we are all fine. Then come straight home. Walk quickly. I'll wait up for you."

Jun nodded to his mother's every word. The cannister fit comfortably into the crux of his arms. It really wasn't heavy, but the container was cumbersome enough to keep him from barrelling down the stairs in his normal fashion. He stepped past the first landing where the Leung's lived. When he reached street level, the outside door moaned its protest at the nocturnal intruder, and then creaked shut. Jun quickened his pace and headed down the deserted street.

Ma-ma sighed. She always sighed when Jun's father and Jun's brothers had to work late. It was a rush order. Spencer's wanted the pillowcases done by the next day for their "White Sale." There was enough stitching and monographing to keep five people busy, but tonight in the drygoods store, there were only three. They could have had three and a half pairs of hands, but when ba-ba and the boys were at the shop, ba-ba preferred to have Jun at home to help ma-ma and to buy the groceries.

She "closed" the kitchen light and followed her shadow, taking the scant steps to the boys' room. Ma-ma peeked in. Their flat, and the one below, were above the key-maker's store. The wooden structure, which shrank and expanded with the changing seasons, was long and narrow. So too were the living accommodations. With only two sleeping rooms, the older boys normally stayed at the shop. Jun and the two younger ones slept in the room just off the kitchen. The sisters said their brothers were "lucky" - particularly when winter brought the biting evenings to their fingers and toes." Not only that," the sisters would exclaim, "but the boys don't have to go nearly as far to the outhouse."

Ma-ma bypassed her room and guided herself around the sleeping girls. Kay, Gum and Hong were nestled in the double bed which took up nearly half of the sitting room. Ma-ma's walking about had begun to disturb the baby. He squirmed and shrugged his shoulders in a tired ache, for ma-ma's back was becoming uncomfortable. She loosened the ties of the straddling cloth to allow for more moving space. The child gurgled and turned the side of its head so that his left cheek now rested behind his mother's shoulder.

"He must be getting hungry too," thought ma-ma. "Men always fuss when they get hungry." As they had done countless times before, knowing fingers instinctively undid the knot which bound the child to its mother. She eased her fourth son to her breast.

Cradling the infant, ma-ma drew herself to the little niche between the window and the wall. During the day, she would stop here in between chores to make sure that the children were within seeing and hearing distance. But tonight, only the dull brightness of the moon illuminated the three-paned window which framed her outside world. The window determined exactly how much of the hustling sidewalk she could see, and how many of her western-clothed countrymen she could count. From here, she could see the boys darting in and out of the grocery stores, herbalist and drygoods shops, trying to remember everything on the check-lists their mama's had mentally inscribed. From here, she could hear the clip-clop of the horse-drawn vegetable carts as she watched small groups of men milling together, exchanging bits of news, cigarettes and laughter.

"Jun should be back shortly. He hasn't far to go ... just to the end of the street."

Ma-ma pulled up the sitting chair and sank gently into the faded floral covered seat. Rarely did she have time for herself. The constant throb of daily chores had ceased for the night. The children had been fed, bathed and now slept. The laundry had been done and the dishes washed. She rested her eyes and reflected on the day. It was like the calm before the storm.

This morning while she was hanging out the laundry on the back line, Chan Mo, her neighbour, told ma-ma about the impending arrival of Lo Lee's third wife.

"Third wife," she had gasped, "Oh, what a tizzy that household must be in. It was difficult enough for this second wife and her children to cope with that mealy-mouthed elder wife! But, who knows, perhaps they could join forces and gang up on her!" chuckled Chan Mo.

Chan Mo delighted in describing, in graphic detail, the goings-on of the other families in the community. She reported on who was doing what to whom, and with whom, when and where. Her children were older than ma-ma's and some had been sent back to China to attend school. And since she could neither read or write, she indulged wholeheartedly in talking - about others. Chan Mo lived in the flat next door. Although several years older, she was ma-ma's closest friend. They had come over on the same boat. Her husband Chan Bak was a good friend of ba-ba's father.

Ma-ma wondered how Lo Lee's young bride must be feeling. She cringed whenever she recalled the blistering July afternoon her mother told her she was to marry a "guest of Gum San."

"You will be well looked after. You'll have many servants and pretty clothes and good food. In Gold Mountain you will be treated like an empress - even better," she had said.

So anxious to have her daughter lead a more hopeful life than herself, ma-ma's mother did not hesitate to let her make the two month journey across the ocean to the land of "Gold Mountain": the "white ghosts" called it Victoria. Ma-ma's own father had gone abroad years earlier to where the "black ghosts" were, but he never came back nor did he send for them. Chan Bak had given ma-ma's mother a handsome bride-price enough to look after her and her younger sister comfortably.

Her husband, she was told, "had all the qualities of a good father. He did not drink, smoke or squander his money, and he was a merchant. For only merchants could afford the luxury of a wife and family." He had paid a five-hundred dollar head tax so that ma-ma could enter the country.

For almost each of her years here, she had had a child to mark its passing. This had given ba-ba much respect among the other men. There were, however, many like Kwong, ba-ba's cousin, who were married men but lived their days as singles with only a remittance receipt from the herbal shop to prove that they were still heads of the families.

The child she now held was sleeping contentedly, its tummy filled with warm milk. As her eyes turned to the tiny bundle, strands of blue-black hair dusted her forehead. She swept them back and brushed her hand along the side of her head, smoothing the wisps back into place. She held the baby closer.

The staccato breathing of her daughters fell into the tranquillity of the hour, that suddenly splintered by the yawning of the lower door. Swift footsteps followed suit, bounding up two steps at a time.

"Jun," she whispered.

"It's me, ma-ma," a voice echoed. "I didn't mean to take so long, but Uncle Kwong was there and he gave us sweets."

"Go to sleep now," was her reply to the boy's explanation.

She sat a bit longer, then got up to go to bed. Tomorrow, in the afternoon, she would send Jun to invite Uncle Kwong for dinner.

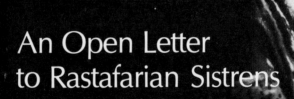

An Open Letter
to Rastafarian Sistrens

Stephanie Martin

Dear Sistrens:

This letter took a long time in coming because I was not sure of its reception or the medium in which to reach you all. Some people might say that this is hardly the place to meet and talk with Rastafarian women because Rastafarian women do not read feminist journals. This might well be so, but I've learnt through the years not to make assumptions about groups of people who have been historically silenced, and who have not had access to the publications of women who write *about* their lives and experiences. My sistrens, we are by no means an exception to this rule, and this is part of the reason why this letter has taken so long. I am hoping, sistrens, that those of you who come across this letter will pass it on to other sistrens who would otherwise not have access to this journal, or who perhaps, under ordinary circumstances would never pick up a feminist journal or magazine that deals specifically with women's issues. This reluctance, my sistrens, is the result of an attitude that we need to work on and eliminate, and that is: the belief that women are their own enemies - that we are gossip mongers - and that the less we have to do with each other the better. Sistrens, we need to go beyond these 'tales.' They have no real basis and are formulated not by us but those whose interest it fits to keep us divided. There are good people and bad people, my sistrens, and they come in both sexes, as experience teaches us; gossip is not an exclusive women's property. Talking to each other about our lives, our problems with brethrens in the movement, our hopes and aspirations, new areas of work that we would like to get into, our vision of a new movement where women and men are equal, does not constitute gossip. On the contrary, talking to each other and sharing aspects of our lives is a way of moving forward, a way of freeing ourselves. My sistrens, we have suffered too long from this conspiracy of silence.

This is a difficult letter to write. There are so many things to say, and yet where does one start? Everytime I pick up my pen a fear stops me which makes me want to water down my words, question my authority and hold back the power in me to express myself. That fear largely derives from our relationship with the larger society. It is a relationship which has always been filled with ambivalence and hostility. Their concept of Rastafarianism is a stereotypic and popular one: 'wild long dreadlocks flying in the air, marijuana addicts who claim that the late Emperor Haile Sellassie is God; and wild mad (wo)men who are constantly in trouble with the law.' There is no denying that our brethrens, more so than us, have felt the brunt of this attack, even within our own black communities. They have been subject to numerous beatings and insults by the babylonian police department, who in their discriminatory enforcement of the law, serve and protect the ruling interests of the society. But my sistrens, although most of us have escaped physical attack we have not escaped degradation and psychological brutalization - for we suffered alongside our brethrens, sharing with them every insult and blow to our collective pride and dignity. We have paid a price for this solidarity, namely, our participation in the conspiracy of silence. It has induced this fear of divisiveness which has paralysed us from speaking, and me in particular from writing before now. In our need for a united front against oppression we have tolerated blind acceptance, which has not only silenced us as women, but has also affected the ability of the movement to move forward as a whole. It is the fear of being accused of disloyalty which has silenced me before now.

We know deep down from the bottom of our hearts that there are internal problems within the movement, and a major one is the treatment of Rastafarian sistrens by Rastafarian brethrens. Yet we don't speak to these issues. Why? Is it because of our antagonistic relationship with the larger society? Or is it some other reason? How do we deal with this internal conflict? Do we sit quietly and fight against racism and imperialism and forget about sexism?

My sistrens we've never talked about this and I've never heard your views on a whole range of women's issues. In our movement the brethrens are the ones who represent us in the media and in books. We are rarely called upon to articulate our position and world view.

It has always been interpreted *for* us rather than *by* us. We have been kept silent and confined to the bedroom, sometimes to the kitchen. We never have the opportunity to speak for ourselves, in clear and coherent voices, about our lives and the meaning of 'Rastafari' in our lives. This letter, my sistrens, is an appeal for us to begin working together to break this silence by coming together to experience the true meaning and understanding of 'collectivity' among Rastafarian people

My sistrens, Rastafari is a unique and beautiful experience:

It is a movement of black people who have recognized that they are Africans, and who have explored and understood the methods necessary to elevate the people of African origin forward to their rightful status nationally and internationally. It is a movement based on the recognition of Africa as the central origin of religious history, culture, science and technology, as well as the modern-day repository of the world's wealth - gold, diamonds, oils, industrial metals. Rastafari teaches love, perfect peace and (the sisterhood) and brotherhood of all people.

The power and influence of Rastafari, particularly through its music, have reached the ears of many of us, especially those of us who have experienced cultural isolation here in North America in all its varied forms. It is refreshing for many of us to find a movement that teaches black pride, African love and at the same time despises both black and white oppressors. What is very painful for me, though, is that in our attempt to recreate and establish our own cultural identity, we've also blindly accepted outmoded ideas about women.

As a black woman/a Rastafarian woman, I know about oppression for I have experienced victimization by both a racist and sexist society, and it hurts and frustrates me to encounter this sexist form of oppression in a cultural identity I've chosen to embrace.

What I'm saying my sistrens is that there are many Rastafarian brethrens today who believe in the subjugation of women; believe that sistrens should be subordinate to them, walk behind them instead of beside them. They also try to tell us that we're unclean during our menstrual cycle. How can we believe this, that something so natural and beautiful can be unclean?

They make decisions for us about birth control and they tell us that if we uncover our locks or choose to wear pants that we have somehow participated in sacrilege. They speak for us and define us as their 'Rastafari queens,' which translates into child-rearers and help-mates. What are we? Don't we have minds of our own? Don't we have the right to make our own choices? To choose whether to be a full-time mother or to choose another career that is equally fulfilling personally and equally useful to the community?

I know too, that there are also many sistrens who have internalized these things and are also guilty of being caught superficially in the cultural trappings of the movement. I have witnessed Rasta sistrens talking about, and ostracizing each other because their skirts were not long enough, their shoes not flat enough, or their head wrap not tied in a special way. I've also been in the company of Rastafarian sistrens who chastise other sisters for not "*Living Up*." What is this "*Living Up*" we speak of ? Let us really think about it, for most times it translates that - if a sister questions 'male authority,' - if a sister thinks for herself - then she is not "*Living Up*."

Is this what Rastafari is about, allowing others (male) to think for us? Are we, then, as the books describe us "passive, docile," always there to serve others, but never concerned about our own needs and what we want out of life? Always being defined by others and internalizing that definition?

As I sit here writing, I remember a discussion that took place about a year and a half ago in the Rastafarian Cultural Workshop (Toronto). In this group discussion there was myself, three other sisters and four brethrens. It was one of those nights that was dubbed "speak your mind," where topics could be introduced and discussed. I remember the discussion started off with individuals sharing their views and opinions on Rastafarian women who wear pants. The general view was that women belonged in skirts and dresses and that only men wore pants. I tried to point out to the brethrens and sistrens that people must have individual choices and that Rastafarianism was a freedom movement, not a bondage movement. I was quickly dismissed as "another one of the black women caught up in this 'white women's libber shit.'"

We then moved on the menstruation. I looked around the room, and thought that at least on this issue the women would be united. I felt sure that the four women would agree with each other and that all the brethrens would agree with each other. But I was in for quite a surprise, because it turned out to be five against three.

One sistren became the spokesperson for the other four brethren, "all women are dirty when they're seeing their period," she said. "I agree with the brethrens here that women shouldn't be allowed to cook during those days, and that they shouldn't go to church either or shop for food items; it's o.k. for her to clean the house, but no cooking....I'm unclean when I'm on my period," she reaffirmed, and the brethrens supported and cheered her on. My shame for her was mingled with shame for myself and the rest of the sisters in the room. Tears were forming in my eyes, and there was silence among the other sistrens. I could argue no more, I got up and left the meeting.

As I write this letter, I'm remembering other instances where brethrens have defined us as inferior and where we've demonstrated how we have internalized this imposed inferiority by our silence. Or did our silence really mask the anger and rage boiling within us?

One such incident took place about ten months ago at a meeting where a group of 'progressive' Rastafarians were planning a cultural show. Close to the end of the meeting, one brethren sighed and then said, "...about the food, I think...a brethren should cook." When another sistren and myself objected, we were overruled by both brethrens and a few sistrens. One Rasta woman said, "I agree a man should cook, because we won't be able to make as much money if a woman cooks, because plenty brethren won't buy the food, they might think the woman is unclean." My shock and shame was great, and even now, I find it hard to articulate exactly how I felt as I was assaulted both as a woman and as a person. For weeks I pondered over the incident and wondered where did these brethren come from. Were they not like me, of woman born? Again, during that incident, I witnessed the silence of my sistrens who did not agree with that line of thought but nevertheless kept quiet.

There are also some of our religious brethren and sistren who will quickly point to the Bible for justification of their treatment of women. I want to ask those sistren and brethren if they can find any passage in the Bible where Jesus Christ was contemptuous towards women, or talked to them in a derogatory fashion. Where is this justification? Aren't we all equal in the sight of God?

When I think about these things I rage inside and I wonder how is it possible that a movement which speaks of liberation, perfect love and fights against black and white oppressors can in turn oppress women. But each time I ponder this, I can't help thinking about how much we have contributed to this view of ourselves, and have let so many things go unchallenged. Yet I know how easy it is to fall into that trap - by virtue of our membership in the movement we are often times isolated from our parents, former friends, etc. And the only place that support is often forthcoming is from our Rastafarian communities; they are a place of solace even with all their problems and complexities.

This letter took five long years in coming. The years when I should have been writing. I found myself locked into a "silence" - a fear of being isolated and rejected, both by Rastafarian sistrens and non-Rastafarian sistrens. On the one hand, I felt that you my (Rasta) sistrens would not choose to identify with my interpretation of our oppression and in turn would deny that it exists. I have also kept silent among my non-Rastafarian 'progressive' sisters because during those years of silence many of them often insulted me by stating that they could not understand why "an intelligent woman" would choose to be a part of a movement that is so oppressive. This question always made me defensive, my sisters, and it must do the same to you at times. How can one begin to describe the dynamism, the magnetism, the sheer joy, the irey-vibes that have captured the hearts of many of us through Rastafari. How can I describe to my sisters that special feeling of belonging, of redefining the meaning of our lives as a people. But perhaps, my sisters, things of the heart cannot be totally understood by others who have not experienced it themselves.

And it is for this reason that I make no apology about the journal which I use to reach you. For we too must be part of that contemporary worldwide movement to redefine the meaning of humanity and personhood. We must join the chorus of voices wherever people are seeking liberation from all kinds of oppression. We have a lot to offer and a lot to gain. Let our voices be heard and let us participate in the creation of a world where not only the colour of a (wo)man's skin will be insignificant but also where the sex of an individual is no barrier to their personal development and their opportunity to contribute to the total development of the race and humanity.

As Rastafarian sistrens, we owe it to ourselves to redefine the movement and our position in it. The movement is not only the brethrens, the movement is us; we are a significant and powerful force. We have the power and the vision to contribute to the charting of Rastafari history. Sisters, we have to begin speaking for ourselves. We have been silenced for so long that now we have to shout loud so our voices will be heard.

My sisters, we can no longer be afraid to speak out, let the chips fall where they may. How can we continue to remain oblivious to the world around us and oblivious to various social revolutions that are taking place and have been brought about by people who are struggling for mental and physical freedom from oppression? There are examples of strong women all around us, women who fight and speak up for their right, women who *know* they are equal to men. Our sisters have waged struggles in Mozambique, Guinea Bissau, Zimbabwe and presently in South Africa. There are women waging struggles all over to be freed from imperialism, sexism and racism. Look at our sisters in Nicaragua and El Salvador. All of these women have struggled beside men and they have been no less effective in bringing down their oppressors. These women have also vigorously struggled with their men about sexism, and have challenged long-standing outmoded attitudes towards women. We have to take up the fight against sexism. I know there are sistrens outside there who are troubled by this dangerous cancerous disease. We need to get rid of it.

I long for change, and I'm getting impatient. I dare to take this thing on, I dare to struggle against it, this thing - sexism. For as long as there is misogyny and sexism in the movement there will continue to be this inner turmoil, and with this inner turmoil, there can be no unity. Where there's oppression and domination there can be no equality - inequality breeds discontent.

My dear sistrens, this letter has been too long, and too long in coming. But there is much to say and the time to say it is now.

Sisterhood and Rasta Love
Makeda

Meena Dhar

The Story of a Birth

Himani Bannerji

The afternoon was very still. The light rested gently on things, seeping into them quietly. The world was brimful of this mellow winter sun. She stretched out her legs and took up the knitting - a soft blue wool, rolled up tightly into a ball. Her hands moved back and forth, the blue line moving in and out of itself. From time to time her belly undulated, rocked by some inner waves. Slowly she dozed off - her hands resting on her lap, the knitting falling onto the ground. But the voices under the window woke her - they came from the waterpump with its narrow trough. She lifted the slats in the green wooden window and peeped out. There they were - all ten of them! She counted one by one, searching for a particular face, and finally found him at the end of the line, laughing, jostling the man in front of him. She moved forward in her cover and raised the slats a little more. But the orange flowering branches of the *golmor* tree blocked her view. With some effort - pulled herself up to the spacious window sill and kneeling there, peered out, breathing heavily. Now she could see the whole of him - a tall man with an ungainly body like a stretched out and knotted piece of juterope - his head thrown back, body arched to receive the water that the guard poured into his mouth from a brass pot chained to the side of the trough. The pot blazed in the sun and the water descended, not liquid but a column of crystal boring into the man's throat. Just then sounded the whistle, jerking back the body into an upright position, and the whole line moved. Adjusting their pace and distance from each other, the men shuffled back, raising the noise of irons and little puffs of dust. And everywhere there was this dust as there had been no rains for a long time. The trees and the bushes were all covered in a red powder, hiding their natural vivid green.

Silence returned with their departure. The pool of sunlight closed in on itself drowning the voices. Only the occasional cry of a vendor or the abrupt and harsh noise of a crow disturbed its calm surface intermittently. She returned to her chair, heavy and lazy, and took up the knitting half-heartedly. The room she sat in was like a vast aquarium in the half-light of which the furniture stood with the fixity and shadowiness of rocks in a sea-scape. The high ceilings, the drawn curtains, the green walls, the dark wooden doors all combined to create this impression. And sitting here, all alone, the cook and the servant having withdrawn to the servants' quarters, she felt that the whole world had fallen asleep. Even the prisoners working all morning in the flower garden had returned to their barracks. This sleeping world would awaken only in the evening when, with the sound of heavy boots crunching down the gravel on the garden walk, the master would return - tired, a little dusty, ready for home and comfort. But for now even she decided to drag herself off to the bed.

Lying in the bed, rocked between sleep and waking, she stared at the design on her bedspread. It hypnotized her. The colours had faded a little, but the print was still clear. It still showed rows and rows of caged birds, two by two, with their beaks touching. Her eyes kept on following the outline of each cage, a trick of her sleepy head, eyes riveted to the strong black outline magnified the size of the cage, while the green and the red birds receded into a great distance. Every time she dozed off she felt that she was about to enter into one of these cages, and woke up with a start. This frightened her. So, abandoning all attempts to sleep, she propped herself up with some pillows and picked up a magazine from the side-table. New books, new plays, new films, every one thought this, that or the other - messages from another world. She read slowly, forcing herself to concentrate, but the baby in her was restless, he would not let her lie peacefully. She knew it was a boy, she had been told so by old women, because it kicked her so hard and moved around in her so unmercifully. And wasn't she wasting away, unable to eat much even at this advanced stage? Right now this angry child was ransacking her belly - it knotted, tightened, hurting her, pulling at all the muscles and the nerves. It was as though he was trying to escape. Slowly she soothed her belly, palm down, rubbing down, slowly calming him, imploring him to wait his time. Gradually the tension subsided - and this knotted, crouching, rebellious mound of humanity relaxed, let go and, she thought, fell asleep. Then she too relaxed and sleep, like fine grains of sand, was running through her eyes and brain, filling up her skull with light, flimsy dryness. Now she wandered in a sand-bank. Strewn with human and animal skulls, bones all half-buried in the sand. The bones were bleached into a fine ivory white, but on many of them the eyes were still intact. They were petrified, glassy and gazed straight ahead of them. She was filled with sheer terror and tried to run away from them but her feet were trapped in the sand and she tripped coming crashing down on her belly. 'My baby,' she screamed, 'my baby,' as she woke up with her heart beating loud and fast.

She decided not to sleep anymore. Her throat felt like a dead well. As she poured some water from a black, burnt-clay pitcher she wondered why time lengthened so much in the afternoons! Now she settled herself again in the living room and picked up the knitting. She wished the servants were back in the house or that her husband would return. Her mind wandered off to her family, far away, and she wondered how her mother was. But no matter what she thought she could not shake off the feelings that her dream had created, and could not forget the look in the stony eyes of the skull. She felt that somewhere long ago in real life she had seen such a look, eyes turned into stones, in a known face that itself had turned to stone. She groped in the dusty corners of memory, lifted curtains, brushed back cobwebs and discovered a tunnel, and entered into that darkness which took her back into a bedroom a long, long time ago and stood staring at the corpse that lay stretched out in front of her. That was her father - or what had been once her father - now turning into stone, gazing with stone eyes into a world where she could not enter. She extended her hand and touched the unblinking lids and slowly eased them down trying to cover the look but the lids resisted. So there he was - dead - conclusively. And she stood in front of this mass of deadness utterly without any comprehension.

All night she kept a vigil in this narrow room, washing the dead, decorating his forehead with sandalwood paste, swaddling him in new white sheets. She watched the clay brown face take on a penumbra of gray. His nostrils became pinched, his cheeks hollow, and his lips a dark purple and slightly pouting without their look of form resolve. She ran her fingers over his face and he felt cool to her touch, and the flesh was hardening, as though it resisted all touch as sheer intrusion. She herself experienced an immense isolation, as though she were enclosed in a fort, her mother's sobs and grandmother's wails howling like the wind around the high walls that he had erected around her with his death. She surveyed the room that contained them - narrow, rectangular, the windows barred, small, medicine bottles on dusty shelves, the yellowing walls, the faded tiles, and she herself, tearless, composed, at one with the corpse in front of her. She heard the sound of a train going by, a metallic gash on the dark spread of the night, the house shivered, a little plaster fell, and slowly the night broke as the earth revolved on its way towards the sun.

The night broke. It crumbled around her - a dark rock worn away by the wailing, the wind and the sun. She felt its dark grains fall like ashes on them - saw him through a gray haze, without arms or legs, buried in the dead debris of the night. A strong wind blew her back to her childhood. She was afraid, she wanted to touch him, to hold his hand, but he was not there. He had drawn a circle around him with his life of violence, and now, that invisible boundary had been etched sharply with the brass relief of death. She waited in this timeless space of neither advancing, nor retreating until the dawn fully arrived. Then came the four brahmins, the cheap wooden bedstead, the flowers, the garlands and the incense. They covered him in flowers, draped him in garlands chanting all the while "only the name of Rama is true. Hare Krishna." At this he rose from the earth. On four sturdy shoulders he left through the southern door, never to return and she followed him out into the world.

Outside the breeze was liquid and cool like a river. The trees were moist green and the poor were waking in their sidewalk homes, rolling up their mats, washing at the hydrants. Trams clanged past sharp and loud, and crows descended on the bits of rice and grain which they scattered as they went down the path of renunciation to that of auspiciousness. "Only the name of Rama..." they chanted and women, in wet clothes on their way back from the holy river, lifted their hands to their foreheads in a gesture of fear and respect. Then they entered the courtyard of the crematorium. "Only the name" ...they breathed and lowered him to the ground. His journey was over. And now the fire and the earth awaited him and also the river in its coolness. The jute stalks and the dry wood were blazing as he lay there upon the logs awaiting consecration by his children. They walked up to him one by one and touched his lips with the lighted brand breaking the timeless and rigid symmetry of that leaden face. Now he burst into flames, shot up to the sky in vivid colours. The skin sizzled, the fat sputtered and the joints crackled. He burnt resplendently as he never did in life, no even in the violent moments of his anger. Even though he had resisted her he communicated perfectly with the elements and relinquished his form to them and left her standing there staring at the ashes, the grime, the charred bones and the earth, looking for a meaning. And none was to be found, only a dissolution, as he cast his charred bits and ashes into the river, becoming one with its ebb and flow, its mud and slime, moving toward some ocean - nameless and formless.

Meena Dhar

On the tenth day came the priests. She sat with them, washed, fasting and in fresh clothes, with little mounds of rice, flowers, sesame seeds in front of her, pouring water from one copper pot into another, floating crimson petals in the little brass vessels. They were little boats sailing off into that other world where he stood in a crowd of ancestors, waiting for this remembrance from the living, the branches and shoots of the tree of genealogy, its roots invisible, buried in the darkness of the past. She, a descendent nourished this tree with her offerings and the same would be done some day by her child, another shoot of that mysterious, massive tree. "Be propitiated," she said to them, repeating after the priest, "We, your descendants, dedicate this to you. You are still among us, remembered by us, we feel your presence, we pity your thirst and agony. Drink this water and be sated, eat this food and be satisfied, take this flower and smell its fragrance, be propitiated." Then rose the voice of the chief priest alone, utterly solitary in the wind, seeking elemental protection for the newly dead, the one reborn now in the past. "Let the earth that receives him be honeyed, let the sky, the air, the earth and the sunshine be filled with sweetness." And the earth, the air and the sunshine responded. The day became a beehive, a heavy sweet golden fruit, and stretched out to the sun, lazy and heavy, into an afternoon such as the present one when she herself a pregnant woman revisited the moment of her father's death, saw him in the womb of time, herself in the womb of her ancestors, and her child in her own womb.

II

The big wall clock over the head of the stairs struck five times. The master would return soon.

It was time for her to get ready. She dragged herself before the mirror. It was hard to recognize herself in that heavy, swollen pod. The face was still same, but with a look of inwardness. She was always listening for some signal from within. She did her hair up in a bun, put a little red dot on her forehead, and changed into a dark red sari, his favorite colour, then went into the kitchen. While she waited for the oil to heat, she looked around the kitchen. Everything seemed alien and unreal; and she asked herself, how did I get here? It was as though she had sleepwalked into an unknown house, in an unknown town and woke up with a stranger in her bed. She continued preparing the meal with this feeling of strangeness hanging over her, until a pain inching its way forward forced her to the present moment. Is it going to happen tonight, she wondered.

The pains came at long intervals. She arranged the food in silver dishes which the maid took to the table. Together and silently they finished their work, and when the maid left the room she went to the pile of letters lying unsorted on the side table and started to separate them out. It seemed very hot in the room, and she wiped her face with the end of her sari, taking care not to smudge the red dot. The house was too silent, she thought. It would be nice to live with more people, or if her husband did not stay away so much. All this living alone is making me very morbid, she thought, getting up to switch on the electric light hanging over the dinner table. Her mother had asked her to go home to have the baby but she had not gone. Who would look after her husband? She had replied. But that was not the real reason. She had not gone because she felt no real contact between herself and the relatives that she had left behind. They too had a shadowy quality about them now - as everything else in her past and present. And besides she was better off here where her husband was taking great care of the mother of his son. The district civil surgeon was always available and a very good mid-wife, good food and medicine as well. Her own poor family, living on the income of her uncle was not a good place for her now.

She sat for a while knitting, heard the iron gate creak on its hinges. Moments later there were footsteps crunching the gravel on the walkway. His peon came in with a basket full of files, and he walked in after, blinking at the bright light near the door. Then he smiled and walked over to where she was sitting and lowered himself into the big leather armchair next to her, and lay back with his eyes closed and legs stretched out in front. She looked at him - his eye lids were still twitching, and there was a fine layer of dust on his brushed back hair. He was a man in his late thirties, tall, wiry with a receding hair line, and fine features which seemed sculpted with great care. The firmness of his jaws was immediately noticeable, as was the unexpected dimple on his chin. His eyes which were now closed were large but heavy-lidded, and further increased the air of withdrawal that surrounded him. He spoke very little, read a great deal, and was altogether unlike the usual notion of a prison warden. He seemed much more to be a man who had withdrawn within the walls of academia. He was not harsh and used corporal punishment very sparingly, and reluctantly. The prisoners respected him and he had done as much as he could to reform the daily life in a prison. He had introduced regular craft classes and higher education, and only this year two prisoners had been awarded with diplomas. He had written forcefully in favour of abandoning the outmoded methods of prison organization left over from the British Raj. He had actually opted to work within the correctional system. And he had been a very successful jailor who had kept people happy even in a prison. This made him a happy man. He was satisfied with his control on them - 'not brute force, but moral force is what we must use,' he said to her very often. In the days of nationalist fervour he was strongly inclined to Gandhism, the trial of will and asceticism that it implied attracted him. Perhaps he would have been a great nationalist leader, she thought, had he been born into a wealthy and well-connected family. As it is he was contented, quiet, efficient and unchallenged in his own line of work. Wherever there was trouble they sent him and he always managed to quieten things down. Everywhere he showed the evidence of foresight, in his own marriage for instance. He had married quite late in life because he had responsibilities to fulfil and a career to build. With such a man, her family had thought, she could never lack security. And they were right. She had been kept very well, well-groomed and well-tended. In his own way he was even a good lover, he made her feel well-used. Now as she watched him, resting in the depths of the armchair, so quiet, so tired, she once more, grudgingly, admitted that he was a good-looking man. Mature, firm, sinewy, any woman might want him. But what nagged at her inside was would he want them? Would he ever, helplessly, powerlessly, surrender himself to anyone, a man or woman, and say without you my life is meaningless? Without you I am incomplete? Many times, lying in his arms, she had said, 'I really want to be with you, I really want to know you,' stressing the 'you' every time. But he had not understood her. 'I am here,' he had said, 'I belong to no other woman but you, no one but you ever touched me in this way. What more can you want? Don't talk so much,' he had said, and made love to her - controlled, powerful, judging her needs, with no awkward movements. She had enjoyed it, but also she stood over herself, watching the love-making with an absent eye, then turned around and looked out through the window at the street lights gleaming on the wet tamarind leaves. All night it rained and she felt in herself the predicament of the patient earth under the insistence of the downpour. The earth like her was controlled, was passive, was to receive what was being given, this insistent bounty of sensations and fertility, this rain.

Now his eyes were open again. He was smiling at her. She handed over the letters to him. He takes good care of his teeth, she thought. After he glanced through some of the letters casually he said, 'I am hungry, let's go to the table.' Now she was playing with the food in her plate, noticing how white and strong his teeth were, how his jaws hung secured by firm wires, and how methodically they opened and closed grinding down the food that she had prepared. He enquired minutely after her health. It was not a casual enquiry - each question was precise and well-informed. Sometimes she was embarrassed by his knowledge of the female anatomy and pregnancy. It was as though she was never to have any secrets from him, even though it was she who bore this child. He wanted to enter her womb with his eyes open, and see and regulate the whole process. When he did this she felt very resentful. She pulled her sari carefully over her body, and looked down at his boots. They were never dusty, never unpolished, she thought. They were also very big and heavy. For a man as tall and wiry as he was, his feet with his boots on looked grotesquely large. He shouldn't wear them indoors, she thought. She wondered too, why he never took them off except when he went to bed. The only time she ever saw him in a rage was when a new servant had left an unpolished patch on one of them. He was immediately fired, and a prisoner, very young and amiable, came in the morning and polished the boots until they shone like mirrors in the morning sun. Then he approached his master, now bathed and fed, sitting in his heavy leather armchair, feet out-stretched to enter the boots. These thoughts drifted through her mind as she sat there listening to him talking at length about the unreasonable expectations of his relatives, about work-ethic. The young, he felt, were having it too easy. His childhood or youth was not like that. No father nor uncle pushed him through, the only son of a widow, he had struggled for his living, succeeded in a small way, had arranged marriages for three sisters and when all his duties were done, then and only then, refusing a dowry on principle, had married, had taken his pleasure, from which he had so long abstained. Now he was waiting for his son, he had duties towards his own family. As she listened the pain grew in her. The baby was no longer moving. He was still and heavy, and hung in her belly, like a bunch of fruit, head downpoised for descent. The pain was not from him but came from way up in her back. It gathered like a wave slowly from quite a long way, endless little currents of pain joined it, increasing the volume, heightening the crest, and crashing down around her hips. She knew that she should speak to her husband about it, and arrange to get to the doctor on time, but her tongue felt paralyzed. She could neither move nor speak, her eyes were riveted to the gathering darkness outside. The light from the window fell upon the prison wall, shining on the branches of the jacaranda trees. The earth was losing heat rapidly and a scent of wet grass drifted in from the freshly watered lawn. This is when her eyes picked up the outline of a man in the act of lowering himself over the prison wall. But she said nothing. She saw him, as one would, a figure on a movie screen, a figure without depth, just an outline. He smiled at her and lifted a hand in greeting and then jumped out of sight. It was he. His smile was unforgettable. He was always smiling and joking around in a loud voice. He had already broken prison a few times and was always brought back, increasing his sentence by a few more years. He was a murderer. He had killed his wife's lover many years ago and never repented. Even now he sent her some money from the prison. She had moved in with another man and had some more children. Everyone knew his story and now he was escaping again. When he dropped out of sight she turned her face to her husband. She was amazed at the man's daring greeting to her, the jailor's wife. Had he known? How could he that day after day she sat on the window-sill, lifting the green slats, watching him work, watching them walk around with the jangle of shackles? Would he kill someone else again she wondered? Should I tell him, she asked herself, and then didn't. The man had trusted her and she kept his trust and waited to see what would happen.

She did not have to wait for long. The evening count of the prisoners had begun - the man was missing. There was a search. He was nowhere to be found, and then the alarm, the five by five clanging of bells began. It brought her husband immediately to his feet. He ran out saying - 'I'll be back soon.' He came back within minutes, got dressed, ordered his jeep and opening his drawer took out a shining new revolver. Then walking over to where she sat, placing a hand on her shoulder, he said, 'I'll be back soon. He can't have gone very far. But don't worry if I am late. Send the maid to the doctor's house if you feel unwell. He'll come immediately.' Suddenly he looked very excited. Sitting where she was she could see his legs, thighs terribly tensed, waiting to spring into action. He is waiting, she thought, like a hound, ready for a chase. The smoke screen had lifted from his eyes leaving them bare and gleaming. He was waiting for her to say something, the revolver hanging from his left hand, a moment before turning around. 'Don't kill him,' she said, unable to stop herself. 'Not if he doesn't try to kill me first,' he replied, 'I suppose,' she responded, 'I suppose...' utterly pointlessly. He turned around. In a flash he was gone - running down the steps. The engine roared to life and the headlights of the jeep hit the heavy dark foliage of a mango tree. They were gone and once again silence filled the house, filled the night. She sat very still thinking some day it was bound to happen to you. How can you run a prison and not expect anyone to escape? She tried to think what she would do in his place - but could not at all. She could not imagine what it was to be inside his mind, what it meant to be him. Instead she thought about the man, what he might be doing now, where he might be. It was a very high wall, she thought. Right now he may be lying on the ground with broken legs. But that wasn't true because then they would have found him now, there would have been voices near the wall. But it was deathly quiet. She moved in to her husband's leather chair. Usually she didn't sit there, but now she was very tired and the pain was so insistent. It was a different kind of pain this time. It was a dry grating pain. It was fixed firmly into her body, like a drill planted into the earth, boring deeper turn by turn, each time more grazing. The waves of pain that came in between were higher now, the distance between them was shorter. She tried to keep her mind off the pain. She followed her husband, a witness to his great chase. She knew where he was going even though it had not been spoken. He and his companions were going to the swamp at the north end of the town. They were almost there, the jeep was moving furiously up a dirt road, grinding the pebbles under its heavy wheels, its lights harsh and blazing on the trees lining the sides of the road. The pain too was moving through her, crushing her waist and legs. The lights in the room were too bright and stark. The jeep moved right into her, crushing all under its heavy wheels and stopped at the edge of the swamp. The men alighted. Four tense silent men stood with their guns ready, flashlights poised, and a familiar voice shouted through a megaphone, 'I promise that you won't be punished if you surrender now. This incident will be forgotten.' No one answered. The four men looked at each other. Their waists were bulging with cartridges, they raised their armed hands defensively and fired. 'Don't try to attack us,' the voice continued, 'we are heavily armed. Don't move from where you are. Surrender.' And again there was no noise, no answer. The pain grew searing as the headlights of the jeep, the flash-lights all bore into her eyes. Pain, she whispered, pain, it's happening. She crouched deeper into the chair, into a hole in the muddy ground, seeking cover, seeking protection. But she could hear them. They had given the prisoner enough time and promise of forgiveness - but he had not complied. The swamp was very quiet. Darkness lay congealed in its hollows, reeds moved with an invisible life, fireflies twinkled and the babies of the water birds awakened by the sound of guns, cried plaintively. A phosphorescent glow hung over the soggy ground and the shallow water which in places was waist deep. The men separated and moved in different directions. She crouched lower, hiding from the pain, from the muffled boot steps, her husband's boots now soiled by the mud. Now she knew why every day, so fastidiously, he brushed them, polished them and refused to part from them. They were the preparation for this moment, this moment of confrontation, of combat with this man in the mud. He stepped firmly and boldly - even on this oozy, slimy ground. He walked with measured steps, calm and controlled. His jaws were set, his chin held high, his eyes bright as torches, he advanced into the swamp, into the hole, into the leather cover, where she sat hiding. Every step he took was lighted. The phosphorus in the stagnant waters sent out streaks of agitated lightning. His legs, now covered with mud, were luminous. His whole being had become an instinct for hunt. He was sniffing for blood, and a strong smell of blood came from the mud. She was wet around her thighs, she was soaked, she was bleeding profusely. Something or somebody had hurt her dreadfully. 'I wish he would stop, if only for a moment,' she said, 'and give me a breathing space.' But he would not, he continued to come towards her, with even steps, attracted by the smell of blood. He was looking for the man, the man who was hiding inside her. She was that vast swamp into which they were shining all those killing lights and shooting randomly. And again she was the man hiding in a hole, and her husband was looking for him or was he looking for the child who was hiding in her? He had come to kill her so that she would yield the child up to him. 'What would you do if I gave him to you?' she said, 'Would you kill him?' 'Not if he didn't try to kill me first,' he replied. His voice had a strange and metallic ring to it. The inside of her head had become a vast dome where the sounds echoed magnified an hundred times. Oh god, she moaned, I am dying, I am all alone. I am being torn apart. I am dying and he still refuses to come. He won't surrender, no even a gun can make him do that. Now she could see the prisoner. He was grinning, showing his strong white teeth. Then he broke into a laugh. He was no longer crouching. As he laughed he raised himself, he stood upright and tall. He threw his head back and out of the red circle of his mouth, wide, ringed by the dark, fleshy lips, came this gigantic laughter - which grew louder and louder. The night shook and jangled with it, the stars were moving at a furious pace, the moon was broken into a thousand fragments. The laughter burned into her like the splinters of a shell, needle sharp rays of the sun. Now her husband had seen them all. Had seen the man, had seen her in her hole, had seen the baby hiding in her. 'Don't move or I'll shoot!,' he said. He came running through the mud, and with one swipe of his hand he laid the man flat on the ground. And he lay there, covering her with his body, one with her, in the mud, in the slime, in the blood. 'Don't!' he pleaded, 'don't master, don't please.' He raised both his hands to ward off the boot, terrible and huge, gleaming with mud, descending, blocking out the world for him. But his hands were too feeble, the boot came crashing down. It went a lightning of pain through her. Something was split open, torn apart. The sound of ripping flesh was everywhere like a piece of cloth tearing. With this mingled a scream, a cry. 'A child is crying somewhere,' she thought, 'in me, near me. The man is dead. He has killed the man. But a child is here. I can hear this child.'

A Poem by **Pam (Afua) Cooper**

The Ribs Factor

You say I came
from your ribs
how could that be?
why can't you see
the reality?
I need you
you need me
but what I truly need
is respect and equality:

Oh can I and I
continue to believe
that old testament story
in this age and livity*?
we should erase it
from our memory.

From mother earth we came,
with Jah as our father.
Into us they breathe
the breath of life:
pure, sacred and true.

I feel the same things
like
you do,
and maybe I want the same things too.
I don't have to see things through your eyes.
What you say
is not always wise,
    do,
let us through our love
find a way to reason out this thing
today.

*Way of life.

SYLLABARIUM

SYLLABARIUM

	PAY	PIN	EE	NO	TOO	PUN	PAN	ENDINGS
	Ā	E-I	Ē	O	OO	U	A	
A								
P								
T								
K								
CH								
M								
N								
S								
SH								
Y								
R								
L								
V								
W								

EXAMPLES

MI NA KI NU TO TU MA TIN

Cooking Bear Meat

Martha Pachano

First you skin the bear. Then you cut the front of the
   bear down the middle.
Then, take all the things inside the bear out.
   First, you cut the front teeth, with three big bones
and take them off. And then the back feet, the same
   with three bones.
Then, cut off the head of the bear. Then you cut along
   the long bone and ribs in the back. Then cut around
the big bone near bottom of the bear.
   That is the part of the bear we put on a string and
cook on an open fire.
   First, you hang the big bone near the fire.
It goes 'round and 'round, 'round and 'round, 'round and
   'round, back and forth many times until it gets brown.

ᐊᖨᑌᐁ ᐯᓯ ᐃᑕ ᒥᐢᔮᐸ

ᓂᔭᒪ ᒥᐦᑐᓄᐟ ᒥᐢᔮᐸ

ᐊᑕᒪᐸ ᒥᐦᑐᐤᐟ ᑕᑕᐁᐸ ᐁᓚᐦᐟ ᐸᐊᓯᑕᐤ

ᒪᐦᓄᐤᐟ ᐃᓂᔦ ᐊᑕᐊᔭᐸ ᐁᒪᐦᔩᐟ

ᐃᓂᔓᐦᑕ ᒥᐯᐁᐧᓯᐯᐧᒣ ᐃᓂ ᐯᔭᐅᔦᐟ

ᐧᑫᐯ ᐁᐊᑕᒪ ᐸᐢᐧᓯᔦᒣ ᐅᔦᐯᐧᒣ

ᐯᐧᔾ ᐊᐁᐯᓄᐯᐧᒣ ᐊᑕᒪᐸ ᐸᓄᔦᑕᐊ ᐤᑫᐯᐧᒣ

ᐊᑕᒪᐸ ᐸᔭᐸᐸᐦᐁᐧᒣ ᐅᔦᐯᐧᒣ ᐸᔮᐸᐦ

ᐃᐢᐊᑕᐸ ᐸᐊᐢᐁ ᐁᐧᒣ

ᐊᑕᒪᐸ ᐸᐃᐨᐊᑕᐁᐧᒣ ᐣᐤᔨᐣ

ᐸ ᐊᐢ ᐸᐁ ᐤᐊᑕᐢᔭᐧᒣ ᐊᑕᒪᐸ

ᐸᐧᐸᔾᐸᐸᐊᐟᐁᒣᐧ ᐟᐸᐧᐁᐤᐟᐸᐧᐅᐧᒣᐟᐸ

ᔾᐸᐣ ᐯᐊᐟᐁᒣᐧ

ᐸᐤ ᐢᐟᐧᐊᐊᐣ ᐸ ᐨᐸ ᐊᑕᐊᔭᐸ ᐤᐊᑕᐊᓅᐟᐁᒣᐧ

How To Cook Indian Pudding

Juliette Iserhoff

8 cups flour
1 lb lard
8 tablespoons baking powder
1 tablespoon salt
1 teaspoon allspice or cinnamon
1 cup currants
1-1/2 cups raisins
6 cups molasses
2 cups white sugar
1 teaspoon salt
5-6 cups water

Before you mix you puddin', put the big pot on the top of the stove.
Fill the pot half full of water and wait until the water is boiling.
Then mix your flour in a big round dish. Then add lard.
Mix flour and lard by your hand. Add baking powder, salt,
raisins, currants, allspice or cinnamon. Then mix molasses,
brown sugar and white sugar in water.
Add this to the first mixture.

Then use a 100 lb flour bag to cook your puddin'.
Tie the bag with a string. Boil for 5 to 6 hours.
About 20 servings.

ᐃᓯᓯᐤ ᐳᑎᐣ

8 ᒥᓂᑳᑭᐟ ᐱᐧᑳᓯᑭ ᒥᑲ

1 ᑎᑐᐸᓴᑯᒋᑭᑕ ᐃᒥ

8 ᐊᒥᑯᐟ ᐅᐱᓯᑲᑕ

1 ᐊᒥᑯᓂᓴ ᒧᐃᑯᑕᐠ ᑲᐱᒋᔅᑎᓂᑲᐠᐃᐠ

1½ ᒥᓂᑲᑭᐟ ᓴᒥᓂᓯᐠ

1½ ᒥᓂᑳᑭᐟ ᓴᒥᓂᓯᐠ ᑲᔦ ᐱᓯᓯᐠ

2 ᒥᓂᑳᑭᐟ ᐅᓴ ᐅᓯᑲᐤ

6 ᒥᓂᑳᑭᓚ ᑲᐧᐃᐸᐠ ᒥᔦᓴᐳ

2 ᒥᓂᑳᑭᓚ ᑲᐧᐃᐸᐠ ᓴᐧᑲᐤ

ᒪᐊᒥᑰᓚ ᓴᐃᑕᑲᓚ

5 ᑲᔦ 6 ᓂᐱ

ᐊᒧᔦ ᒋᔅᐳᐅᑕᒋᐳᑎᓚᒪ

ᒐᑕᒋᔅᑕᔦᓚᒋᐳᑎᓂᓴᒌᑯ

ᒐᐊᐱᑐᔅᒋᓚ ᐸᒋᔅᑕᔦᓂᐱ

ᐊᑯᐃᔦᓚ ᒌᒋᔅᐳᐅᑕᒋᐳᑎᓚᒪ ᐊᒥᔅᒐ

ᐅᔦᑭᓚ ᒐᐱᒋᔅᑎᓂᑐᐤ

ᐱᒐᓯᑭᓂ ᑲᔦ ᐱᒥ ᑲᔦ ᐅᐱᓯᑲᓚ

ᑲᔦ ᓴ ᐃᐧᑕᑲᓚ ᑲᔦ ᓴᒥᓂᓯᑲ

ᑲᔦ ᒐᐧᐃᐸᒐ ᒥᔦᓴᐳᐃᑲᔦ ᑲᐋᐸᒼ ᓴᑳᐤ

ᐊᑯᐧᐃᔦᒐ ᒐᐱᒋᔅᑎᓂᐟ ᐱᒧᔦᓂᐠ

ᒐᒪᑯᐱᑎᒥᓚ ᐱᓴᑭᓚᐱᔅᒪ

ᒌᒋᐸᐱᑲᑎᑕ ᐊᑯᐧᐃᔦ ᒌᐱᑭᓯᑐᐧᐋᐅᑕ

ᒋᐳᑎᓂᓴᑯᒐ

ᒐᐅᓴᐅᑕ 5 ᑲᔦ 6 ᐊᒋᓂᑳᑲᓂ ᑕᐟ ᐱᕈᒧᑲᓚ

ᐊᔦ ᐱᐠ ᑲᑕ ᐃᓴᐱᔦᐤ 20 ᐊᒫᐄᑲᓂᐃᓚ

Fish Soup

Juliette Iserhoff

First clean the fish, if you have four medium
  sized fish,
Cut your fish in four or five pieces.
  Then put in pot to boil for one hour or less.
Put half water in cooking pot.
  Then if you think your fish is done or cooked
take all the bones from the fish
  Then smash it and put it in the pot.
The pot that you used to cook you fish in, of course,
  and then you use the same water.
Let it boil for one hour more.
  Then you mix a little flour into a mixing bowl.
Then water, and put this into the cooking pot to
  thicken the soup.
This makes six or eight servings.
  Of course you can put salt or pepper in if you wish.

ᓂᒫᒉ ᐊᐸᐋᐳᐁ
ᓂᔅᐧᔦ ᒫ ᒑᓄᐳᐢᐧᔦ ᒫᓂᐧᒪᐧᒪ ᐊᔭᐳᐧᐊ ᐋᐧᒐᐧᔦᐨ
ᒍᐁ ᐊᔭᔅᐣᐣᐟ ᓂᒫᐧᒪ
ᐊᒐ ᐊᔦᐧ ᒪᒪᐣᐧᐤᐧᒉᐤ ᐁᐊᐤ ᐧᒥᔨᓂᔭᐧᔨᐨᐧᒥᒉᐧᒐᐧᒐ
ᐊᒐ ᐊᔦᐧ ᒪᓂᒉᔨᓄᐧᒉ ᐊᔅᒡᐧᔦ ᒉᓂᔥᐳᐣ ᒡᐳᐧᒉᐧ
ᐊᐣᔭᔅ ᒉᒐᐸ ᒉᔅᐧᒐᐊᐁ ᒉᐣᒉᓄᐧᐊᓄᔅᒉᔨ
ᐧᔭᒍᐤ ᐊᔦᓄᐧᐁᐧᐨᐁ ᐣᒉᒐᐸᐧᔥᐊᔅᐣᐧᒐᐧᐊᒌᐧᒡ
ᐊᐣᔦ ᐊ ᐊᒉᐧᒐᐳᒉᐨ
ᐊᒉ ᐊᐣᒉᐧᒉ ᐊᐣᐳᔅᐧᐊᒍᐊᔨᐧᔦ ᒉ ᐊᒉᐳᐧᐨᐧᔥᐧᒉ
ᐊᒐ ᐊᔨᐧᔦ ᒪᐳᐣᐧᒉᔨᐨᐧᒉ ᒥᔨᐊ
ᔥᐧᒥ ᒪᒡᒪ ᐳᒍᐋᐧᒉ
ᐊᒍᔨᐧᒉ ᒪᐣᔥᔨᐧᒉᐧᒐᐧᒉ ᐊᐧᒉ ᒐᔨᐧᔥᐳᐳᐧᐨᐨᐁᐧᒉ
ᒉᐣᒉᐧᐊ ᐊᐧᒐᐧᐧᒉᐧᒐᐧᒪᒪᐧᒐᐧᐧᒐᐧᒉᐧᐤ
ᐊᒐ ᐊᔨᐧᐊᒉ ᒪᐣᐳᔅᐧᒐᐧᐊᐧᒐᐧᐧᐟᐤᐧᒐ ᒉ ᐳᒪᐊᒡ ᐊᒐ ᐳᔨᐧᐊᐳᔨ
ᔥᐁ ᒪᐳᒡ ᐧᔦᔥᐧᐁᐧ ᐊᔥᐧᐨ ᓄᐧᒐᐧᐧᒉᐧᐨ ᐣᔨᐟᒉ
ᐊᒐ ᐊᔦᐧ ᒪᒉᔥᐣᐳᐣ ᐊ ᐳᐧᐨᐧᔥᐳᔨᐳᐧᐧᐤᒪᐧᒐᒍᐧᒉᐧᐨ
ᐳ ᐨᐧᒉᐧᔨ ᐊᐧᒐᐧᒪᒉᐧᐊ ᐧᒉᔨ ᒪᐣᐧᒉᔨᐧᒐᐧᐧᐤᒉᐧᒐ
ᔫᐊᐧᒉᐧᐧᒐ ᒉᔨᐧᒐᐧᐧᒉᐧᐊ
ᒉ ᒉᔨ 8 ᒪᒐᐊᔨ ᐣᔨᐧ ᐧᒉᐧᒐᐧᒐᐧᔥ

Pieces of our lives

On the Bus

Desiree Hinkson

All the seats on the bus were occupied except for one at the back. I made my way to the back and sat down. I ran my fingers through my hair, trying unsuccessfully to put it back into place. The Afro had some ideas if its own, refusing to budge, it stuck out in various directions. The fatigue made my eyelids heavy, so I snuggled back into the semi-comfortable seat. As I was beginning to get settled and comfy, the aches that had been building up all day began to hurt. The headache that had been threatening to come, came. My toes were straining rather painfully against my shoes. I longed for the comfort of my bed. And to top that off, my tweed skirt was beginning to make me itch. I longed to soak in a warm tub. I must have dozed off for a bit because I jumped when I heard some voice yell: "Get down tonight baby! Yeah! Yah!"

I turned in the direction of the noise. In back of me there were two Black boys with a gigantic radio, snapping their fingers to a repetitious beat. I stared hard at both of them. They ignored me and kept on moving to the beat of the music. I turned around in my seat with my back to them again and tried to ignore the music.

Looking around I noticed that the music was bothering other people. I began to watch them closely. A man across the aisle from me was trying to ignore the noise. He was tapping his feet in a nervous staccato. He looked at me, then looked away. The old woman beside him was looking at the boys with something close to hatred in her eyes. She was moving her lips in an angry manner. But no sound came from those lips. Now and then people would look to the back and look away. Resentment and anger visibly clear in their glances.

The man across the aisle looked resentfully at the Black boys; then he looked at me. It wasn't no ordinary look. First he looked at my feet and then continued up my body until his insolent eyes were level with mine. He didn't look into my eyes, he turned his gaze away abruptly. I knew that type of look. I'd seen it all my life. I hated it. I'd seen how it had stripped good men and women of their dignity. I wasn't about to become another victim. I raised my chin and stared back at him. "Screw you too," I thought silently while my eyes were relaying the same message. The silent battle went on. He must have done this often because his eyes didn't budge from mine. I was an amateur at this but I wasn't backing down because hell, it was my pride on the line.

His stare began to waver. "You gutless chicken," I thought nastily, as he tried the feet-to-eyes stare. I did the same but curled my lips in disgust. He turned his gaze to the boys at the back, then he turned back to me. He looked at both of us in indecision.

In silent battles such as this one you have two choices; either you fight till the finish or back down and be scarred for life. I had been scarred too many times. I wasn't going to be a victim this time; I wanted to be the one who did the inflicting. Suddenly he turned to the Black boys and said: "Turn off that damn music!"

This new tactic caught me off guard. I looked at the boys to see how they would react. "Be strong," I prayed silently. One of the boys turned down the radio, then addressed the man in the aisle.

"It's a free world mister and if I want to play my music, I can, so fuck you," said the boy slowly.

I could've jumped for joy. Normally I got upset when youngsters were disrespectful, but this was an exception. Then the man said, "All you stinking niggers are alike."

There wasn't a sound on the bus. Everyone was waiting for someone to answer. I looked at the man and gave him an evil and superior smile. "That's right we all stink," I said to him pausing to make sure that I had his full attention. "Just like your momma."

There was an audible gasp from the old woman beside him. She looked at me but didn't say anything. I wished she had because I was on a roll. I could have taken on the whole Ku Klux Klan right there and then. The man's hands clenched and unclenched. I could feel the violence and hatred in him. He didn't respond to my insult. He got up and walked to the front of the bus and got off at the next stop.

The Black boys turned the volume of the radio back up. I looked at them without saying anything, then I turned back and snuggled down in my semi-comfortable seat. I dozed off to the sound of "Baby get down tonight."

A Story To Tell

I've got a little story to tell you. It's about me. I've got a little difference to share with you. It's about you and me.

We live in the same community and are oppressed in some of the same ways, but we don't all necessarily recognize oppression as oppression. Some of us claim to be more oppressed then others; some of us blame others for being oppressed. I don't think that there is any point in saying that one is more oppressed than another, for being a woman brings oppression, being a feminist brings oppression, being Black brings oppression, and being a Black lesbian brings oppression.

My story that I have to share with you is about being a Black Lesbian Feminist.

I have lived in three different countries in my life. The country that had the most influence on me was the United States. That was where I discovered my true lesbianism, gained my independence as a woman and had my first taste of racism. At the time, I was in love and living with a white woman. We lived together as lesbians but spent little time together in public, because we couldn't express ourselves, and because of racial tension in the United States. When we did go out together, we were usually faced with hostility. We went shopping a few times in clothing stores, and the sales people would communicate only with my friend, pretending that I didn't exist. This also happened in restaurants. I remember we once sat together in a restaurant waiting to be served for quite a long time - longer than people who had come in after us. I remember being very upset and that I complained to the manager who told me quite rudely to leave if the service was not good enough. That was my first real confrontation with racism in the United States. It was only one of several such incidents.

We both had separate friends. My Black American friends would often put me down for spending time with, what they called, "white trash," and her white friends caller her "nigger lover."

We rarely talked about racism. We pretended that it did not exist. We were in love at the time and that was enough. We tried moving to other states but found that racism existed there also. I was really frustrated and finally gave up and moved back to Canada. That was five years ago. During those five years, I discovered that racism existed everywhere.

It was difficult to emerge in the Black community here in Toronto as a lesbian feminist. My family and Black friends saw me as being different. We lived in two separate worlds. With them, I share Black oppression, and with my lesbian friends, I share lesbian oppression.

As a lesbian, I was not accepted in the Black community. I was forced to make friends in the white lesbian feminist community. I found out that a lot of white women who are lesbians don't know how to accept Black lesbians. Because of this, they usually make a lot of racist comments or jokes. Once, I was sitting with a group of white lesbians and we were talking about how we came out as lesbians; they asked their white friends, "How did you come out?" and when it was my turn, one response was "How come you are a Black lesbian?" - as if it was unusual to be a Black lesbian, as if all Blacks are heterosexuals. In their company, they make me feel as if I am a zombie. They expect me to relate to their white culture, to understand it and accept it. But if I start to talk about my culture, then the conversation dies, or the topic changes or no questions are asked.

I usually experience a lot of racism from white women and sometimes wonder if they are aware of it. Several times, white women have told me, "We really like you because you don't act Black." That frustrates me. I can't afford to settle for such a narrow definition of myself. In the past, I have tolerated it, saying to myself that these are my lesbian friends with whom I share one form of oppression, but it took me quite a while to realize that simply because I was a Black lesbian, it did not mean that I had to tolerate their racism. I realized that what I shared with these women was a dual identification which forced me into making choices that were not always right, but which were necessary at the time, i.e. immersing myself in the white feminist community without them accepting me as a Black lesbian because I felt so isolated from the Black community.

But I am learning to deal with the issue of racism in the lesbian feminist community and the prejudice against Black lesbians in the Black community. I am learning that I do have a choice as to how I most want to be identified, and that is as a Black Lesbian Feminist.

A Woman From Interval House

I never went out alone. I was always with him. My husband would always lock me up. He would go to work and take the house keys with him and I couldn't go out. Even after I had the baby I had to stay in the house. When he came home from work he would take me and the baby out, like to the park, or for a ride in the car. Then he would drive us back home.

After being in the transition house away from him, I just don't think I could live like that again.

I'm from Fiji where I lived on a farm with my brothers and sisters and my mother and father. We kept cows and horses and planted sugar cane and other things. I went to school there and lived in a village of about five hundred people. All the people lived very close together.

I was nineteen when I got married, three months after I came here from Fiji.

I had a boyfriend in Fiji, and I wanted to get married to him because I loved him. My parents didn't want me to get married to him because he was lower than us in the caste system. I don't believe in that but my parents do, and that's why I was sent to Canada to my brothers. I remember that I didn't like Canada, and I told my brothers that I wanted to go back, but they said no. They said they had found a very nice boy for me to get married to. That is the way it is in our custom. If your parents or older brothers say you have to get married to someone, you've got to do it.

Before I got married to my husband I saw him a couple of times, but I never talked to him. He came to the house a couple of times, to visit my family but not me. Like, we sat down in the same room and we had coffee. But when I looked at him, he wouldn't look at me. It was weird because what I thought my marriage would be like was completely different from what I had. I thought that I would know the guy. I wanted to get to find out what he's like, what he wants, what I could do to please him. With my husband, I didn't know anything. He was about ten years older than me. He was so quiet and I couldn't just go and talk to him with everyone around because then they'd say that "This girl is so forward; she's just doing things her own way." It's not expected of girls to do that. Men are supposed to make the first move! (laughs).

The first time I talked to him was my wedding day, and all we said was "Hi." I had nothing to do with the preparation for the wedding. My mom and family did everything. My mom even bought my wedding dress. She came to Canada for the wedding. I kept telling everyone that I didn't want to get married, but they wouldn't listen. So I had no choice. So I got married....

For the first couple of months, my husband was nice to me. He wouldn't really beat me up until the first anniversary of our marriage.

I stayed with my husband for two and a half years. In between those two and a half years, I left him about three or four times. I would go to stay in a number of transition houses in B.C. My baby was four months old when I left my husband. I left him because he would mentally abuse me, beat me up; he would stay out late at night running around with other women; then he would come home and accuse *me* of having affairs with other men, accuse me of the things he was doing outside! It was always this mental cruelty: he would always tell me that *I* was crazy. I didn't think I could take anymore so I just *had* to leave him. I talked to my husband a couple of times and told him that he had problems and that he should go and get help and he agreed to do it. He was going to counselling, and I thought he would change, but then he started telling lies. He started telling my family that I was having affairs with men. I said I wasn't doing that! I was in a transition house where you are not supposed to go out with men and it's very strict. You have to come back to the house around eleven o'clock. You can't stay overnight anywhere! I realized that if he was like that when I was in a transition house, he would never change.

I called my husband and I told him that I didn't want to go back to him, that I wanted a divorce. "That's it," I told him. "You are out telling lies about me, that's it. I'm not going to give you the chance to hurt me anymore." When I started divorce proceedings, he found out where I was living. He found out where the transition house was.

I don't know whether he told his brothers to do it, or his brothers just did it, but they actually tried to kill me. They had a gun with them. One day I was at a shopping mall and when I looked around I saw them in the car. They were following me everywhere I went. I would go into one store and the car would be parked in the parking lot; then I would go to another store and the car would be parked in another parking lot. It was always there, I always saw it. I was so scared. I don't even know how I made it back to the transition house, I was so afraid. The next thing I know my husband calls my social worker and tells her that his brothers are looking for her to kill *her.* That same night, I was moved from that transition house to another.

My brother called the house to tell me that my husband was following them and swearing at them. I called my husband and I said, "Why are you doing that? If you want to do something, do it to me!" And he said, "Oh yes I'm going to do it to you, because I know where you're staying." And I said, "How do you know where I'm staying?" Then he tells me, "Oh, you went to London Drugs on Monday, and then to McDonald's, and then you went to a couple other stores." And I said, "How do you know that?" because that was exactly what I did. And then he said, "I'm going to kill you and I'm going to blow the house up." I knew I couldn't stay in B.C. because then I would have to stay in the house all the time and be scared all the time. You know, scared that he might somehow come there, or that I might run into him somewhere.

The first time I came into a transition house, I didn't know what it was. In Fiji, we don't have such places where women can go to if they are beaten up by their husbands. When I came I found that I had a room of my own, and that there were people there that I could talk to, and who could talk to me, about my problem. Talking always helped me; it helped me to face up to my problems and to think more about my life. I found most of the counsellors would say things to make me feel better and to make me feel strong, and do things for me. The interval house is like a collective. If we want to go to a movie, there is morning and afternoon child care. I went out a couple of nights ago to see an Indian movie. I was feeling so homesick and alone that I went so that it could cheer me up.

If the book I wrote is a success in Fiji, then maybe I'll go into journalism. The book was about Canada in general, and about transition houses and my experience in them. When I worked on the book I really enjoyed it. It was something I wanted to do and nobody forced me to do it. I didn't have to answer to anyone: it was mine, my baby, and I did it, and I felt good about it. I think it would really help women in Fiji, because if they read it, they could see what things are being done in Canada with women, and they would try to change things in Fiji. I most definitely think that the women in Fiji need these things, perhaps much more than women here.

Presently, I'm enrolled in a self-defense course, because I heard that my husband knows I'm here in Toronto. I don't want to be scared of him anymore, or anybody else! I want to be able to protect myself and my baby.

Obasan by Joy Kogawa

Lester and Orpen Dennys Ltd.: Toronto, 1981

Kerri Sakamoto

Obasan powerfully recounts the story of the Japanese Canadians during World War II through the eyes of a young and sensitive girl, Naomi Nakane. What is most moving and impressive about this novel is Joy Kogawa's ability to subtly and delicately give voice to an essentially voiceless people, the Issei, to whom the book is dedicated. The portrayal is such that in no way does it violate the dignity of their stoicism and humility.

Through this novel the Issei, the Nisei and the Sansei speak out at last - that is the first, second and third generation Japanese Canadians - all those whose lives were irreversibly affected by the persecution which resulted in the confiscation of their property and their eventual internment in concentration camps in the British Columbian interior. The spirit of the Nisei is embodied in Naomi's Aunt Emily, the civil rights crusader. Hers is the meticulously documented, orderly and rational expression of anger and outrage. Her manuscript entitled, "The Story of the Nisei in Canada: A Struggle for Liberty" opens with the following words: "I understand the Nisei." She tells Naomi:

The power of government, Nomi. Power. See how palpable it is? They took away the land, the stores, the businesses, the boats, the houses - everything. Broke up our families, told us who we could see, where we could live, what we could do, what time we could leave our houses, censored our letters, exiled us for no crime.

Naomi's uncle remarks that the Nisei are not very Japanese-like, that they are "muzukashi" - difficult people - unlike the Issei who do not like to talk about their victimization. But Aunt Emily's outspokenness is very necessary. Not only to speak of injustice but also to proclaim vehemently, "For better or worse, *I am Canadian.*" For Naomi she is the vital link to her mother, to her inherent Japaneseness. It is Aunt Emily who tells Naomi that one cannot simply "turn the page and move on" for "the past is the future."

As a grown woman, Naomi reads Emily's manuscript upon the death of her beloved Uncle and she is drawn into her past and beyond. Naomi feels the heaviness of the book with voices from the past - "a connection to Mother and Grandma Kato I did not know existed." Her remembrances of her mother from whom she is separated before the bombing of Pearl Harbour, are tender and filled with longing. Although Naomi is very young when her mother leaves to return to Japan, Naomi has already learned from her the language of silence. Joy Kogawa lets this silence speak poignantly with genuinely poetic imagery. The essence of the Issei spirit is captured in their hushed whispering in the face of their adversity: "Kodomo no tame - for the sake of the children - gaman shi masho - let us endure." It is this characteristic of serene and quiet acceptance of life - the Japanese often call it "mono no aware" - which Kogawa portrays so beautifully.

The inner calm in the eye of the storm seems all the more remarkable because of the schizophrenic nature of their very exist-ence as Japanese Canadians. As Obasan (Naomi's Issei aunt) prepares for their departure from their home, Naomi notices her packing away "Mickey Mouse plates and rice bowls in layers of comics crumpling them all together." It is this schizophrenia which Naomi must come to terms with. And in order to do so, she must acknowledge the past, she must be told that which the silent voices denied her knowing. In the most devastating passages of the novel, Naomi at last learns about her mother's agonizing death in Nagasaki. She is compelled to speak out to her: "Gentle Mother, we were lost together in our silences. Our wordlessness was our mutual destruction." But still Naomi recognizes the beauty of "dormant blooms," of the "forest braille"; she bids her loved ones to "rest in your world of stone" as she acknowledges the importance of remem-bering the past. We too must do the same by reading *Obasan*, undeniably a book whose power is such that one cannot simply turn its pages and move on.

Primitive Offensive by Dionne Brand

Williams-Wallace International Inc., 1982. 59 pps.

Himani Bannerji

> Dessalines you were right
> I can hear that cry of yours
> ripping through that night,
> night of privateers
> night of fat planters
> leave nothing
> leave nothing white behind you
> Toussaint heard too late
> when it was cold in Joux.
> (Canto VII, p.41)

> dead things weigh me down
> this obsidian plain
> bald
> dead things
> dead leaves
> dead hair
> dead nails
> tongue, a swollen flower
> glottis, choked with roots
> (Canto IV, p. 14)

I don't know any other way of describing Dionne Brand and her poetry except by saying that she is always ahead of, as well as trying to catch up with, herself. And catching up, as we know, is a hard matter, implying being late, being in a hurry, and for a black Caribbean immigrant woman, it means catching up with the past to sense out the present in order to seize the future. Of course, this means a journey, not an abstract journey through an abstract time, but a populated time filled with the cumulative experiences of those who went before her, suspended by the concrete contradictions of the present moment. Thus, Dionne has to perform a very complicated set of movements - runs, gropings, gyrations, wrestlings, hand combats, and ritual dances - all so that she can move back and forth, up and down, all at once.

This is how she has to place herself, in her own place, which is also the place of her people. The history of the Caribbean people, indeed of all colonized people, becomes one with the search for her own being. In this enterprise, Dionne is alone, because her subjectivity is the starting point of the exploration.

When you decide
you are alone
when you dance
its on your own
broken face
when you eat
your own plate of stones
for blasted sure
you are alone

(Canto III, p.8)

But then, she is also intensely accompanied because she has consented to inherit, to taste, all that her ancestors have left her: shit, tears, blood, bitterness death, rage, and a combative love that rouses her to defend her people. These are the elements that compose the personality of Dionne - the descendent of slaves, indentured workers, migrant workers, runaway slaves and freedom fighters. She picks up as weapons two adjectives that the imperialists have labelled her with - 'primitive' and offensive' - and hurls them back at her oppressors as a call to war. She has accepted her status of being 'primitive.' Through an act of reinterpretation, she has rid the word of its imperialist, pejorative connotations, and returned it to its meaning as the originals, the essential, the ancient and the basic. By reworking the word 'offensive,' she is now ready to strike the first blow. The days of black defensiveness are certainly over. This then, in a nutshell, is the content of Dionne's new book, a long poem in cantos, entitled Primitive Offensive. In this theme she is not original, and that is her strength, for she keeps company with the best black writers that we have.

Primitive Offensive is a book of war, a book of strategies and tactics, a book about countering the violence of domination in order to set right the violent world order created by imperialism, colonization and slavery. it is a violent poem, for as Fanon[1] says, decolonization is a violent affair. Dionne declares her intention when she says:

> I went to Paris
> to where shortarsed Napoleon said,
> 'get that nigger Toussaint,'
> Toussaint, who was too gentle,
> He should have met Dessalines,
> I went there to start a war
> for the wars we never started
> to burn the Code Noir
> on the Champs Elysees
> (Canto VI, p. 32)

The poem stretches itself on a canvas frame of contradictions, oppositions and inversions because the world order of the slaver, the imperialist, is one of bizarre distortions.

> some solar-winged brutal contraption,
> with another columbus aboard
> another Santa Maria perhaps
> another De las Casas
> another slavery
> will surprise me
> consorting with a boa constrictor.
> (Canto V, p. 29)

The world of De las Casas has swallowed up the world of the colonized people - negating their life and meaning with one stroke of the sword and the pen. And this lost world must be reassembled first, piece by piece, as are the shards of 'the ancient African potters':

> I pored over these
> like a palaeontologist
> I dusted them
> like an
> archaeologist
> (Canto II, p. 12)

Nothing that can be used will be thrown away.

> I will
> take
> any evidence of me
> even that carved
> in the sky
>
> (Canto III, p. 13)

And then this inverted world must be set back on its own base; the negation must be negated. The way to accomplish this task is to go back in time, to seek out the lost steps back to the first moment of encounter with the whites, the moment of the Fall, as it were. For the colonized people, the records of that time are not to be found in the official textbooks of history, or the archival records. Rather, an appeal must be made to memory, to the oral tradition persistent among the oppressed people. So, an invocation is in order to an ancient spirit, who must speak in the sybiline and oracular tongue - an ancient medicine woman. It is with this ancient spirit that the young rebellious woman, the poet, must merge in order to know what actually happened. And what actually happened is a long nightmare of history, heaps of death, loss and corruption. And yet the chains must be re-worn and each instrument of torture must be recounted, recounting the terrible passage from Africa to the new world. All this so that we and our children may know, may remember and in that knowledge grow stronger - 'only when I remember I find myself.' An incomplete must be acknowledged in oneself and history - 'Dismembered woman, truncated continent',' - so that a new wholeness may be found.

A death must be acknowledged so that the dead may be laid to rest and life may return to its ordinariness. The long night of terror of South African apartheid must be lived through into:

> a morning in Pretoria
> a morning nervous and yellowish
> its guts ripped out
> and putrifying
> stuffed back into its throat
> The professor and the national party
> and Botha
> and Oppenheimer the diamond man
> were skeptical about
> the Bantu in Bothutapswana
> goodnight from Pretoria
>
> (Canto XII, p. 53)

And so the liberation, the revolution of Cuba might shine the stronger, and be the herald of a bigger black revolution: "havana twinkles/defiant, frightening,/all the lights are on" (Canto VII, p. 36). One must see in the beaten spirit of the other black people the image of one's defeated self.

One must acknowledge how tired one is, how lost and how alone, of an evening in an empty apartment in the metropolis of the world. One must also congratulate oneself because just to be alive, to survive, is an act of heroism. But from this fact of basic meagre survival, ability to continue no matter what - "I can eat stone/and oil/I can eat barbed wire/... I can grow fat/on split atoms" (Canto V, p. 27) - one must learn a lesson in courage and optimism. As one progresses witnessing the history of one's people, one must learn from the past never to make the same mistakes in one's own strategies of war.

People must carry on this war against colonization, must move on, must run away from submission towards the moment of combat, performed ceremoniously in the spirit of one's ancestors, blessed by Ogun[2] in a ritual dance of war because domination is not the final truth.

> but to be a bright and violent thing
> to tear up that miserable sound
> in my ear
> I run
> my legs can keep going
> my belly is wind.
> (Canto XIV, p. 59)

The tradition of long poems is on the wane. Epics are rarely attempted, so an attempt at a long poem, especially when it is successful, fills one with admiration. Long poems require much more than feelings or an ability to catalyze these feelings into strong moving images. They often require a lot of thinking, a sense of history and/or philosophy. They require a coherent, articulated world-view, and an ability to create a sustainedly interesting narrative since one cannot possibly live through a hundred pages or so of climactic moments. Dionne's work is accomplished on all these scores. She has managed to rework the history of slavery and after into poetry. One can taste, smell, feel the gold and the blood of primitive accumulation on the pages of her book. She has kept an extensive narrative in balance and order by her world view which sees human consciousness as socio-historically produced, and therefore susceptible to change. She has guided us through these turmoil-filled times of history with her politics, which moves from domination to revolution through the agency of a conscious subject. And finally, as a craftswoman of narrative, she has created and sustained our interest through the pages with her strong sense of drama, through the use of vignettes, of constellations of images, of leit-motifs.

The last word on this poem is about Dionne as a woman writer. Two things come to mind immediately. Women, far less frequently than men, have undertaken to create long philosophical poems. Only women poets of recent decades, such as Adrienne Rich, have turned the tradition around. It is a great thing to see a woman pick up this mode and succeed in it. The other point is that, by and large, our experience of colonization and imperialism has been dominantly described and analyzed by men.

Angela Davis and other black women are beginning to set the balance right in the last decade or so. While there is much in common between the experiences of men and women, one could still venture to say that there are specificities to women's experience, even within the same zone of domination. The sympathetic male anger and description of rape, use and humiliation of women, of the invaded, of the subjugated people, does not convey the particular quality of the women's own experience. In Dionne's poem we find this missing voice of a woman protagonist recounting the history of horrors inflicted upon the women before her, on herself, and appealing to her ancestresses.

[1]Distinguished black psychiatrist, author, and spokesman of the Algerian revolution.
[2]Ogun is a Yoruba god of war.

Contributors' Notes

Himani Bannerji was a guest collective member of the *Fireweed, Women of Colour* issue. She is a professor at York University, teaching women in development and third world studies, on gender race and class. She is doing research on colonialism and class formation in India and has been writing a lot on these issues. She is a poet and on the editorial board of Resources for Feminist research, U. of T.

   Dionne Brand was a guest collective member of the Fireweed, Women of Colour issue. She was born in the Caribbean and has lived in Toronto for the last 18 years. She studied English and Philosophy at the University of Toronto and is currently doing post-graduate work at the Ontario Institute for Studies in Education (O.I.S.E.) Brand has produced five books of poetry and one book of short stories. Her poems have been published in various anthologies.

   Ayanna Black is actively involved in the women's community and the art scene around Toronto. She is a poet and writer. Her most recent book is No *Contingencies.*

   Afua Cooper is a poet living and working in Toronto. Her poems have appeared in several anthologies and she has recorded her poetry on two record anthologies. *Red Caterpillar on College Street* is Afua's second book of poetry. These days Afua spends her time exploring Black Canadian History and taking care of her son Akil.

   Meena Dhar lives in Toronto. She is a graphic artist.

   Anita Gore was born in Delhi and grew up in India. She came to Canada in 1979.

   Cecelia Green is a native of Dominica. Her political and research interests lie in the theory and practice of national, Black, and women's liberation and the transition to socialism, particularly in the Third World.

   Nila Gupta, co-managing editor of the *Fireweed, Women of Colour* issue and a past Fireweed collective member is currently working in a collective that is developing housing for women of colour and their children in Toronto. She is still writing sporadically and holding on to her dream of being a film maker. She is part Québecoise and part East Indian and made whole by it all.

   Sylvia Hamilton was born in Nova Scotia where she attended Acadia University in Wolville to study English and Sociology for her B.A. She has spent a considerable amount of time doing research on the social and cultural history of Blacks in Nova Scotia. In addition she has done many years of volunteer work in Black community organizations and community health groups.

   Claire Harris came to Canada from Trinidad in 1966. She is a poet and teaches English.

   Desiree Hinkson was born in Barbados and came to Canada when she was three years old and still considers herself a Bajan first, Canadian second. This is the first time she has ever submitted any of her work for publication. Her story was based on an incident that happened to her on a bus. She is proud of it because it explains itself.

Prabha Khosla was born in Tororo, Uganda. She is presently working in Mozambique. She was a guest collective member of the *Fireweed, Women of Colour* issue.

Suniti Namajoshi was born in Bombay, India in 1941. She is a writer.

Stephanie Martin is an artist/photographer. Born in Jamaica, she has been in Toronto for twenty years.

Dora Nipp is a fourth generation Chinese-Canadian. She was born in Prince George and grew up in Vancouver, British Columbia.

Karen Pheasant is thirty-three years old. She was a delegate to the National Native Women's Health Conference (held in Toronto in June 1973) which focused on children, families and culture.

Donna Phillip is an Oneida form the Iroquois confederacy. She has been involved with the Native Women's Association since 1973. She belongs to a nation which is matriarchal and feels strongly that discrimination against Native women must be abolished. She is the mother of seven children and at times, finds it taxing to be away from her family. However, she will continue to stay involved in Native women's issues and Native Politics in general until the Constitutional issues are resolved by the Canadian government.

Judith Pilowsky-Santos came to Canada in 1976, in exile from Chile.

Claire Preito is a Black woman from the West Indies. She is a film-maker living in Toronto. Claire Preito and **Roger McTair** worked together on the collection of photographs featured in this issue entitled Images of Black women. He is a writer, director, film-maker and photographer who is active in the Black community.

Clarita Roja is a Filipina revolutionary and one of the most distinguished militant writers in the Philippines. Her poems have been published in various journals and her book of poetry *A Comrade is as Precious as a Rice Seedling* was published by Kitchen Table Press.

Kerri Naomi Sakamoto is a graduate of the University of Toronto. She is a writer.

Dee September was born in Cape Town, South Africa and emigrated to Canada in 1961, settling in Winnipeg, Manitoba.

Makeda Silvera co-managing editor of the *Fireweed, Women of Colour* issue, is a writer and activist in Toronto.

Esmeralda Thornhill who hails from Montreal, is an accomplished linguist in English, French and Spanish, a poet, teacher, and Human Rights Educator and lawyer who is also a founding member of the National Congress of Black Women of Canada and the International Resource Network for Women of African Descent (RNWAD)